ABDUCTED & LOST

Diana Linn

dlp

DEDICATION

This book is especially dedicated to my husband, Dr. Robert T. Linn. During the months it took me to write this story that in part I started in my mind many decades ago but had only written a few pages until now. He was my reader, encourager as I passionately wrote on.

Copyright © 2016 by Diana E. Linn

All rights reserved. No part of this publication may be reproduced, distributed, or transmitted in any form or by any means, including photocopying, recording, or other electronic or mechanical methods, without the prior written permission of the publisher, except in the case of brief quotations embodied in critical reviews and certain other noncommercial uses permitted by copyright law. For permission requests, write to the publisher, addressed "Attention: Permissions Coordinator," at the address below.

Please Note: Names and places are purely fictional. Should there be resemblances in past history, it is coincidental.

Diana Linn's Publishing, LLC
6398 S. Wheaton Dr.
Tucson AZ 85747

Ordering Information:

Sales

For details, contact the publisher at the address above. Copies may be purchased via e-mail: bdlinn@icloud.com

Printed in the United States of America

Category of the Book: Christian Murder Mystery. Narrative with a message.

ISBN 978-0-9980819-2-2
First Edition

FORWARD

A note from the author. Other books authored by Diana E. Linn such as *Can Anyone Tell me* is a novel written with a message. It doesn't matter where we are in our lives we can step out and allow God to help us change our destination.

What If ... The Romanov Dynasty a novel as told to the author, is a historical recap in the time when Russian propaganda was at its worst. Research shows that on numerous occasions fact was actually propaganda. Further research shows that the demise of the Romanov Dynasty could very well have become the "Great Escape" of that decade. Thus, the Novel, *What If ... The Romanov Dynasty*.

This novel, *Abducted and Lost,* is a murder mystery written with a message. Written so that the reader can experience how God makes the path straight.

.

PREFACE

Abducted is a novel written with a distinct message. On the one hand life can lead us down the wrong path because of our choices and still God can deliver. We may have to endure the scars but He can set us free if we resolve to follow Him. Though underserving as we are, yet, if we do a turn around the impossible becomes the possible. "... *with God all things are possible.*"

CONTENTS

Dedication

Copyright Page

Forward

Preface

Chapter

1	God, Where Are You	—	1
2	Wondering	—	5
3	Air France	—	11
4	Plans Conceived	—	17
5	The Heist	—	27
6	The Storm Rages On	—	39
7	Pay the Fine	—	44
8	Spain	—	49
9	Mexico City	—	53
10	Dust & Wind	—	58
11	The Delivery	—	62
12	Fire Power	—	66
13	On the Farm	—	71
14	Hiding Baby	—	76
15	Time Moves On	—	80
16	The Search Begins	—	84
17	Trek to Chicago	—	87
18	Slipped BY	—	91
19	Traversing the Plaines	—	96
20	Searching Chicago	—	101
21	Drug Bust	—	105
22	Investigation	—	109

23	The Idea Man	— 113
24	Melville High	— 117
25	Coffee Shop	— 121
26	On the Grounds	— 124
27	The Dance	— 127
28	Church	— 131
29	Meetings	— 135
30	Piece of the Puzzle	— 141
31	The Outfield	— 144
32	The Chicago Scene	— 148
33	Searching High Schools	— 152
34	Preparations	— 156
35	Where is Tabatha	— 159
36	The Party	— 163
37	Tuesday Morning	— 169
38	Running	— 174
39	At the House	— 178
40	The Coast is Clear	— 181
41	The Documents	— 185
42	The Set Up	— 191
43	The Escape	— 194
44	End of the Row	— 197
45	Nearing the Goal	— 202
46	The Story	— 205
47	The Fire	— 209
48	The Future	— 214

Chapter One
God Where Are You?

"God where are you? It's so dark ... I can't move."
Lying motionless, Anita's body felt frozen, she couldn't move a muscle, not even a whisper would pass through her throat. Yet, every bone ached as she hovered in and out of consciousness. Yet, she could feel the presence of people hovering over her body.
"What do you think, Doctor Turner?"
"It's just too early to know."
"How long shall we keep her?"
"We'll keep her to the end, Lydia. I want to give her time. She might come to and then again she might not but I couldn't live with myself if we didn't give her long enough to decide if she wants to fight for life."
"You're saying she can make that choice?"
"God only knows."
Anita heard every word but it felt like a dream but she couldn't respond. Her mouth wouldn't open. It seemed so black but her eyes wouldn't open. Was she blind?

A couple of strangers walked into the hospital shelter dressed in white painting overalls. They looked the part.
"Excuse me nurse, but I heard there was some kind of a car accident in the desert and I thought someone said there were two dead. Do you know anything about them?"
"We don't have any auto accident victims."

"Surely, border patrol would have brought them here, it's the only hospital around."

"Sir, I would need some kind of ID from you if you want information."

"We don't have anything with us."

"What's your relationship to these supposed victims of an auto accident?"

"None, we just read the newspaper this morning. Thought maybe we could help if both of them lived through that incident."

"Both?"

"The Newspaper says there were two."

"First of all, we don't have any auto accident victims but I still couldn't tell you anything if you aren't related. I'm sure if you went to the police station, they would know."

"But, the paper clearly says one was deceased and the other very critical." Here's the headlines," he handed the nurse the morning paper. So that means at least the man died, but we want to know if the lady, Anita, did she die as well?"

"Sorry, I know none of that sounds good, does it?" Nurse Lydia began reading the article. "If you read it all, it says they were gunned down, it wasn't a car accident at all."

"Gunned down? Suppose I didn't read it all, did you Sam?"

"Didn't see that part, George. We thought it was an accident with a late model Jeep."

"Where you men witnesses to any of it?"

"No but we were just in this neighborhood on a job when we bought the papers and saw the headlines. We'd like to help and thought surely this hospital, being a shelter, you would tell us if they were both still alive."

"I will tell you what, why don't you leave your names and contact information so that we could have someone contact you."

"That's all right, we'd just like to see the lady and talk with her if she came through the incident alive and tell her we can help financially."

The nurse continued, "If you really want to help, I can get the director of the hospital to talk with you."

With a blank stare, the strangers nudged one another.

The nurse continued, "There always is cost involved in these situations and since we are non-profit, I'm certain our director of the

hospital would like to talk with you both. They would appreciate any help you can give them."

"Sorry we just wanted to talk with Anton if he was still alive and especially Anita."

"You know their names?"

Ignoring the nurse, the men continued, "But, George the paper says the man is dead, so it would only be Anita and she is too critical to make it, right Nurse?"

"Again, I can't tell you anything, but the Doctor could maybe assist you."

"We have to be going, you've told us enough."

They left.

Nurse Lydia turned almost collided with Dr. Turner.

"Oh, Doctor, I didn't know you were there."

"I was and I heard what they said. Strange, they know her name. We will need to have the local police keep a watch should they return."

"Did you notice their first names were George and Sam?"

"We'll report that. It could be a lead."

It all began back when Anita was feeling restless. Foster care for her had ended because of her age and now she needed to forge her own way. Going to College for an orphan wasn't going to be an option in her part of the world. It had become time for her to figure plans for the future. She had wanted to locate her birth mother but that quickly ran into a dead end. Working as a bar maid to eke out a living seemed all there was. That wasn't really what she wanted t to do that for the rest of her life. She was restless.

Chapter Two
Wandering

    From the Western Harbor of Vastra Hamnen, Anita Bergin could see the stunning view of the long Oresund Bridge, arching its way over to the coastline of Denmark. Visibility was clear but Anita's mind wasn't focused. It was as though she was absorbed in a shroud of misty fog. Today she wandered over to the Luftkastellet lookout point where the sights were even more stunning. The summer months were the best part of the year for Anita to enjoy beach life in Malmo on the South coast of Sweden. That's why she was here. That's why she lingered at this place, to get herself motivated. To create an interest in something beyond herself.

    Sweden is a very long country, coupled with the higher altitudes of the mountainous regions to the North. Northern areas experience snowfall for eight months a year, with temperatures that can drop to below zero for around 184 days a year, compared to 120 days in Stockholm and just 71 days in the South.

    In the depths of winter, the Stockholm area has only around five and a half days of light hours, while in the north of Lapland, the sun peeks above the horizon to give just 4 hours of twilight and almost 20 hours of complete darkness.

    But the darkness is short-lived. Toward February and March, the light returns, bringing with it a combination of winter with the warm early spring sunshine and longer hours of daylight. Even in deepest winter, the darkness is offset by the thick blanket of snow which covers the land throughout the winter months.

In the southern part of the country, winters are milder and less predictable. In southern Sweden, average temperatures in January may be just around freezing, and it is less common for the sea waters around the coast to freeze.

On the East coast of Sweden, the coastal waters of the Baltic Sea between Sweden on its western edge and Finland to the East, regularly freeze. The sea ice, as well as the thousands of lakes dispersed throughout the interior of the country is where ice skating is a hugely popular pastime for all ages.

"Hey, Guys, would you be taking your boat to Stora Karlso?" inquired Anita.

Two seasoned fishermen were busily laying fishing nets down and were about to work on a nearby outrigger. "You want to go there?"

"I do."

"Jump on board."

It wasn't long before they pulled up alongside the dock at Stora Karlso. "Thanks guys." Anita jumped off the boat and walked up the sandy beach.

Stora Karlso is a Swedish Island in the Baltic Sea, situated about six kilometers west of Gotland. Gotland, Sweden's largest island is fully encompassed by the Baltic Sea. If Anita would have been interested in fossil finding, it would've been like a gold mine for her. Yet, it was more of an inner quest to find out where her future would take her. She had that burning feeling in her very soul, *'why am I here anyhow?'*

It was refreshing to sit, watching the waves come and go as they splashed against logs lying about. Anita lay on the beach in her jeans with her blue shirt half buttoned down in front as she dug her hands into the damp sand, turning to stare at the cliffs behind her. They seemed to beckon a dare for an impossible climb. No harness, no protection, but she was bored. *I can do it, and if not?* But her thoughts would not compute in her cognizance.

Anita's mind was made up. Walking over to the edge of the rocky mountain formation, she shook off the sand that stuck to her sandals. Gazing upward at the sharp peaks she took a deep breath. *I'm going to do this.* It was obvious that some noble mountaineer in centuries past had hewn a stone staircase for a few hundred feet upward. *This will be easy. I can just walk up these stairs.* Scaling from rock to rock, she had persuaded herself to go beyond the staircase. She was sure the view would be even better higher, worth the risk. *Oh I know, I shouldn't do this, but I will.* Clinging to the edge, she began the climb upward. Holding on to the jutted stones with her bare hands, she began climbing the rocky cliff face. *A little higher, I must climb a little higher.*

Anita continued the incline until her body wanted no more. She was tired and needed to rest for a bit. Bending down to sit on a narrow ledge she couldn't help but gaze at the scenery. Immersing herself in the spectacular cityscape outstretched, surrounded by mountains her thoughts gave way to thinking, *if only I could stay here.* Yet, she knew she would tire quickly if her hesitation lasted too long. Back to the climb and a few feet higher. Again she rested. Tilting her body slightly, she felt it too awesome to ignore. Looking down on the waves splashing against the sand on the beach, it was breath taking. There it was again, that feeling. *Funny, I keep asking myself 'why am I here anyhow?'*

Anita was a tall slim blue-eyed blonde Swedish gal. She was convinced she was alone with her thoughts. That nagging feeling persisted, *why am I here? It seemed to* become more intense and unrelenting. Her thoughts would not be subdued. Making a sudden turn to gaze at the beauty, the rocks beneath her began to crumble. Reaching into the crevices, attempting to grab anything that jutted upward, yet instead, she slipped further downward. Her sandals slid off her feet as she began the involuntary decent, scrapping her hands, arms and knees while still skidding along the side of the rugged cliff. *My knees, they're bleeding. If only I can grab a rock somehow and steady myself. Oh God, I'm slipping farther. If I yell, there is no one to hear me. I'm actually going to die. God, please help me!*

From out of nowhere and seeing no one, she could hear a voice. She was convinced her mind was playing tricks on her. She shook her head. The voice persisted, "What in the world are you doing, lady?" Grabbing Anita by the arm, "You're going to kill yourself climbing these cliffs and in bare feet. No hiking boots? I can't believe you. Here, let me belt you to my harness. I'll bring you down to the beach."

They made the descent to the bottom. With both feet on the ground, Anita turned to see who had just saved her life. "I was trying to get to the to the top. I wanted to see the view from up there."

"Oh really? You climbed up in bare feet? You know better than that. If I hadn't come along, what would have happened and how did you plan to come back down again?"

"Didn't really think about that but it's so peaceful looking over the water from up there."

"From the beach you can see how peaceful it is."

"Look, my sandals. They landed in the sand, can you believe that?"

The stranger didn't answer, he stood looking at Anita as she hooked in with his glance. Without speaking words, they continued frozen until finally, "By the way, my name is Anton Rosander."

"Anita Bergin, just call me Anita. I can't believe you just rescued me. Did God send you?"

"Not sure what you're talking about but this is where we need to enjoy the view, on the beach."

Anton and Anita felt the warm misty breeze blowing on them, both knowing soon the winter winds would roll in over the ocean. "Why are you here? Vacation?" asked Anita.

"No, I'm just wondering about. Sometimes I work and occasionally hike into the mountains. Go skiing now and then. Do you ski?"

"Have done."

Anton looked down at Anita's feet. "I still can't believe you. Wearing Sandals to climb a mountain and then a rugged one like this."

"Foolish, huh? They are comfortable, you must admit."

"That's just senseless, you know that."

"I know that but why are you here, Anton, why am I here?"

"I've done a lot of wandering about but recently I've decided it's much too cold in the winter for me to stay here."

"The only thing anyone can do in Sweden's winter, in my opinion, is ski. Don't know how you manage but I'm getting restless, I need to go somewhere different, like you just said, Anton."

"No family?"

"I don't. You?"

"Never did know them. They dropped me off at an Orphanage promising to come back. I must've been about five when I heard them say Dad would come back when he could afford me but that never happened. Somehow I shut the rest of his memory out of my mind. From then on I never cared."

"Mine were in and out of my life until it didn't matter either. They could have died for all I know. Maybe they did, who knows. When I was little I'd ask the orphanage but they weren't talking. So much for orphanages, huh? Not long ago I tried to find my mother but I hit a dead end. No family, so why not wonder about?"

"Exactly, Anita, why don't you join me?"

"Where are you off to now?"

"Where it isn't necessarily winter all the time."

"How about in the south of France?"

"Hadn't thought about that but it is an idea."

"Sorry, Anton, I came in with some fishermen with an outrigger but I'm not sure when the guys will return to take us back to the mainland."

"Not to worry, I have a boat tied up at the beach. We can use that one."

From there it was just the two of them drifting from place to place. Sometimes sleeping on the beach and other times finding local hostels. Both of them found work tending bar, pouring drinks for the lonely, tired and sometimes angry people. It was always on a temporary basis. If the job became a nuisance, they would travel to another location.

Anita was drying the last dish at the local hostel when she asked, "Did you ever want to settle down, Anton?"

"Actually, no, I like finding a few days' work in a bar, then grab my paycheck and leave for another town."

"Funny, that's exactly how I feel. Always want to go, almost as if I have to go." Anita asked, "Did you ever think there was a reason for anything?"

"Never sure, but then I'm never anywhere long enough to find out."

So it continued for Anton and Anita. They went from place to place to see what was accessible to them. That is, until today.

They sat at a table outside the local coffee house drinking coffee, "Anita I'm thinking."

"Yeah, what about?"

"We've seen all there is to see here, as beautiful as it is but soon it will be winter. That means cold weather. Why don't we get our travel documents together and go see the world?" There was a detectible hint of excitement in Anton's voice.

"Sounds like a plan." Anita's countenance brightened up. "Like you say, the winter is coming and we've had enough of that for now.

France it is, here we come. Do you think we can just go there and do what we've been doing here?"

"Well, that depends. Why don't we make a plan for our lives?"

"And that would be?"

"In my mind I have a visual scene of us settling down in the States, the US. What do you think, Anita?"

"The United States, you mean in the Americas? Now you're talking my language but with what? We've probably squandered what little we had. I know that people need some kind of financial means to permanently live there. They don't just accept anyone legally without means."

"I wasn't planning on asking permission to live there. I was thinking more like we just do it. Really, when you think about it, we've never stayed in one spot very long for anyone to be interested in us. Nobody cares for us because nobody knows us. In my thinking if we go and visit and just never come back."

"That might be true, but if we want to settle in the US, I don't know how we can. Visiting it like we do in Europe is entirely different there. Settling down costs money."

"We're not quite penniless. I've been saving and I think we have enough to get our legal paperwork and a little more to make that possible."

"Now that you have my attention, why don't we make our first stop France?" It had been Anita's dream to wander around France. "We both speak English and Spanish fluently."

"Do you speak French, Anita?"

"Oui."

"Well, then, let's work on the rest of our lives."

"Let's do it."

In and out of the immigration office was becoming a bore to Anton. "I wish we didn't have to do this."

"I know. Without a passport we can't even get on or off an airplane anymore. Supposed to be for our protection, Anton, and it might be a lot of red tape but it is what it is, so let's get it done."

"We aren't applying to any country to settle in, we're only getting passports so we can visit. That's what I don't like about having to comply. It's such a nuisance."

Chapter Three
Air France

    Anton and Anita stood in line to purchase the boarding passes at Arlanda International Swedish airport near Stockholm. It is one of the largest of four airports located in the Sigtuna, Municipality of Sweden, near the town of Marsta. The name *Arlanda* is derived from Arland, an old name for the parish Arlinghundra where the airport is situated. The "*a*" was added in analogy with other Swedish place names ending with *'land,'* making a play on the Swedish verb which means "*to land."* It was from this airport that Anita and Anton decided they would fly to France.

    It wasn't long before they were able to board their flight. "What are the numbers we have?"

    "16A & 16B. Here we are Anita. Let's get comfortable." They sat in their seats waiting for the *fasten your seat belts,* light to go off so that they could move about. Suddenly and abruptly from nowhere a scuffle started as three male passengers stormed the cockpit.

    Anita asked, "What's that about?"

    "Don't know. Just shut up and don't say anything." They froze in their seats, slipping low, keeping their eyes to the floor of the plane.

    The hijackers pounded open the cockpit door. Within seconds the perpetrators had taken control. Overcome by body slams, the pilot slumped over the wheel. Immediately the copilot toggled the switch connecting to the tower then slammed the plane into automatic. Another hijacker began shouting orders.

"Sir, we don't have the fuel. I'll take it to the nearest airport and you can make your demands there." Within minutes the Co-Pilot turned the plane's wings and headed for the nearest local airport as he began the decent.

"What do you think you are doing?" The hijacker had his revolver jammed in his back. "Sorry Sir, that's all the fuel we have, we can't make it to your destination."

The landing was smooth enough but the tension of not knowing what could happen next was felt throughout the cabin. The hijacker's entire conversation had been echoed throughout the entire cabin but also the tower upon the landing of the Boeing 727. The Co-Pilot handed the mike to the hijacker. "Speak and they will hear."

While the demands were being made the Marshall's immediately boarded the flight. What seemed to be an eternity was only minutes as one hijacker had been overcome. The others were cuffed and led out. "Who's on the stretcher?" Anita sat there in disbelief.

"I think it's the pilot." Another passenger answered. "I thought my *number* was up for sure."

"You and me both."

Anita was sure, "God saved us again."

"I'd like to believe the Marshall's did the job quite well." Anton wasn't on familiar ground with anything about God.

The passengers could be heard sighing in relief as they watched hijackers being cuffed and taken out on the tarmac into patrol cars. The Marshall's re-boarded the aircraft and began the inquisition to identify the passengers as they filed out with hands in the air. They needed witnesses to the perpetrators but also sure there were not more hijackers on board. It took a few hours before the passengers were released from the tarmac.

"I don't know, Anton. Should've stayed in Sweden to mind our own business. I wasn't ready for that."

"None of us were."

"We could've been killed."

"We weren't."

"You still want to go to France?"

"Of course. Can't happen twice."

The world was not on high alert to any degree since this was 1993 and though aircraft were hijacked from time to time it wasn't common place. Often times their demands were met with little or no consequences. However, in some cases passengers were affected and sometimes killed, perhaps because they would dare to speak out against the perpetrators.

"Let's check in for another flight."

"Really, Anton, I don't know if I can do that now."

Trying to stay calm, Anton said, "That was over so fast, Anita. All they ever do is hijack the air craft and force the pilot to go to another country."

"Let's just sit for a bit, wait a minute before we talk to the attendant at the counter. You know as well as I do, they do kill some of the people and neither you nor I know what comes next."

"You don't have to worry anymore, they've been arrested and taken to prison. We'll be okay."

"Up for coffee, Anton?"

"Yeah."

A half hour passed as they sat in the coffee bar were conversations were buzzing about the hijacking. "Have you heard?"

Anton wanted to know. "We were on that Air France Flight."

"You were? Glad to see you're here. Anyone get hurt?"

"The pilot was. Don't know how bad."

"If you heard the news, the reporter said that there was another flight just days ago where four hijackers planned to crash into the Eiffel Tower in central Paris. They murdered three passengers when commandos stormed the plane in Marseilles. They killed the hijackers and freed the rest of the passengers."

"Where did you hear all that?"

"I have a small transistor radio I always carry with me. At least it is over but sorry for those passengers. To think, that flight I just missed by an hour. First I had a flat tire and then I got caught in traffic. I was cussing myself out all the way in. Believe me, I told God I was so sorry but so grateful that He saved my life."

"I'm still shaken from this hijacking. I freeze just thinking we have to board another flight to get to France. It'll take me a bit to get over this one."

They waited for a few hours, when Anton insisted they check to have their tickets updated to fly to France.

Anton checked at the boarding counter with the intent to apologize waiting so long before checking in.

"No need, you are very fortunate you weren't hurt. Another flight was hijacked two days ago."

"We heard."

"We just talked with another passenger who was supposed to be on that flight. How do they get onto these flights with firearms?"

"I've said that more than once. But this is 1993 and I don't think they've figured out what to do yet."

"That's unfortunate if you ask me. I predict it will get worse and then maybe they'll start taking this stuff more serious. For now, we're told to take the money, issue the boarding pass and be sure to ask if they have always been in possession of their belongings the whole time. We can ask nothing more and nothing less."

"Who wouldn't answer yes to that?"

"The bad guy has a different agenda."

Anton couldn't resist saying, "We don't get it, do we?"

The attendant continued, "It wouldn't have mattered this time anyhow, they just barged in and onto the flight. I couldn't even say anything before the door was slammed closed. Joe and I just stood here looking at one another. We called the pilot but I guess it was too late once they had boarded. Not a lot we could do but everyone in our airline knew it was going down."

"Don't worry, Anton, eventually we will get it. We will learn, mark my words." Anita was sure of that.

"With all this happening, is there another flight we can get on?"

"None of our other aircraft have been affected accept that no more flights will be taking off for the United States for the moment."

"I didn't know we booked for the US either, I thought our flight was to go to France." Anton and Anita looked at one another. "We could have been going there?"

She chuckled. "No, that flight wasn't supposed to go to the US, but anytime something goes down, they go on watch because the threat for them could be greater."

"I think we are ready to board right now."

It wasn't going to be easy but both Anton and Anita sat in their assigned seats trying to relax. The flight continued on to its destination without any further commotion. It wasn't long before they were about to land at the Monte Carlo International Airport when Anita asked, "Where to from here?"

"We'll find a hotel, see if our restlessness will leave."

"It's Christmas Eve, Anton. We need to celebrate our first Christmas together. What do you want to do?"

"Doesn't matter to me."

"Let's just enjoy the Christmas decorations and go to a nice restaurant for dinner. I'd like that."

"Let's do that then. It will be a little warmer for us and that is what I wanted. Tired of the cold weather."

The two of them wondered the streets for a bit with their backpacks intact looking at every store window they could find.

"Anton, there's a restaurant." Sitting comfortably, chatting as the wind seemed to wave the tree branches gently back and forth. The weather was reasonably pleasant. After dinner, they walked down the main street looking for a hotel.

"Let's try this one. It seems it won't be too expensive but I hope it will be clean."

After a very restful night, Anita awoke with excitement. "Are you awake, Anton?"

"I wasn't."

"Let's go and tour the town."

"Hold on there. First we need to find work at a bar."

"Yes, but we can tour the town between job searching."

"Let's check out the local bar and see what they can do for us."

"There it is Anton. Look, *Taverne*."

"Hey, you guys, any kind of work for a few wanderers?"

The bar tender turned to them, "You looking?"

"We are."

"Then you're both hired. You can put your stuff in the back room and start right now."

It wasn't long before they had secured an apartment. For Anita, it was all about character even though they had to walk four flights of stairs in a building a few hundred years old.

"What do you think, Anton? We should be able to keep in shape walking four flights of stairs?"

"It is a good studio suite and not expensive."

"I like the character of an old apartment building and it's in the center of town. Only thing is, Anton, I'm not crazy about the wall colors. I think I'll paint and redecorate these rooms."

"Why would you do that Anita? It's not ours."

"Just because we are living here. Might be nice for the next tenant."

"I think you're crazy. The next people mean nothing to us."

"So, in the first place, I'd do it for us."

Anita redecorated the apartment in just a few days. However, she was more excited about seeing the sights of town. Just as Anton had said, the apartment proved to be close to their jobs and accessible to sight-seeing. From working to exploring, it was an easy time for them as they wondered about. Anita had insisted on seeing the Eiffel Tower though she had to travel to Paris to see it.

"The way I see it, Anita, Nice has plenty for us to see."

"But the Eiffel Tower is a 'must see.' People come from all over the world just to see it. I've got to see it and I want to see a lot more than just that, I'll have you know."

Still, it was not Anton's intention to stay long enough to enjoy much of his surroundings.

Chapter Four
Plans Conceived

Every day on his way to work Anton stopped to gaze in the window of a local jewelry store. *How I'd love to buy a ring for Anita. Then I could propose to her.* Day after day, as Anton cycled his way to work, he'd stop at an exclusive fine jewelry store to gaze at the beautiful jewelry. *I need just one. I need the ring.*

He had to go check it out. Just maybe he could buy it. He entered the store in his normal working attire which consisted of jeans, crew neck T-shirt and sneakers but he was comfortable. He had taken on the grunge fashion. However, this wasn't the "Yuppie" generation any more but there was the carryover with Ladies and men dressed to accentuate "Yuppie" style of the 80s. These people had the distinguished look, clearly people of influence.

The jeweler's look penetrated Anton's awareness. *Wow, I see, but my money is all they should care about.* Still, it was that look from the jeweler he didn't like. Once more, Anton looked down at his clothing and then gazed back at the clientele in the store. *Okay.* He decided to ignore his immediate situation, making his way to the counter. He wanted to look and inquire.

It was obvious to the jeweler that Anton was out of his element and determined he didn't need to be in his store.

"I'm sorry, young man. I don't think you can afford these."

"I merely want to know what that ring in the corner costs, Sir?"

"Whom are you employed with?"

"And that matters?"

"These are very precious diamonds. Especially hand crafted and aren't inexpensive."

"I understand. You just said you didn't think I could afford what I wanted for my girl?"

"Maybe someday, Sir, I'm sorry."

"Believe me, I too am sorry."

Anton left, rejected. It had never occurred to him that he wasn't even good enough to make a purchase in a jewelry store. *How dare that man think I'm not worthy? I'll buy that ring if it's the last thing I do. Anita is worth every franc I have and I want to marry her.* His heart ached as he sat in the nearby park. He loved her and didn't want to lose her. *I found her and I saved her life. I don't ever want her to disappear. I don't think I could live without her.* This was such a strange feeling for him. He had spent all of his adult life depending on no one, doing whatever he wanted whenever. Now this? His body trembled as he realized the jeweler might be right. *My working in a bar will never get me what I want. There has to be a better way. I can't give up, there has to be a way, a better way.*

Anton's mind was unrelenting. He couldn't stop thinking about how to work out getting that ring. It would take him forever at the rate he was going. He had no special skills so how could he improve himself? There had to be some way but how? He stopped yet again as he cycled past the jewelry store lingering to gaze through the window. In his mind, he'd say, *why not just take it? It wouldn't even bother me knowing the jeweler is such a snob. How dare he profile me! He might be correct in thinking that but how dare him say that to me.*

Should I spring a surprise entry into the store at closing? Pretend I have a loaded rifle. Wonder if I could do that? Probably would get caught. There has to be a way. I'm not willing to kill anyone, I'm not a murderer so how can I do that without killing anyone and still be able to pull off a heist?

It became a daily event for Anton to cycle and look in the store window. *I've just got to change how I look.* He knew well enough if anyone spotted him, he could be recognized and watched so he wore different hats and jackets to confuse the issue.

Finally, the jeweler realized this man would never leave so he came out to talk with Anton. "Sir, you come by often and look through the window. Maybe we can negotiate something you can afford. I'll show you what we have that might interest you."

Anton thought, *So much for my disguise.* He felt disgusted. Now the jeweler was being the nice guy. *How can I a pull anything off if he's going to be decent to me? Was Anita's thinking God could control even a situation like this? I don't think so. That's just not possible, there's no God who would care about me. I don't care about Him so why would He be interested in me?*

"I'll just be on my way but I promise Sir, it won't be long and I'll be ready."

"This lady you speak of must be very special."

"Oh she is indeed. I will be back."

Anton decided he had done enough watching the store but now he would have to do that from afar. The next day he stopped a half block away from the store, still watching people come and go with purchased items. *I'd never rob the people. I'm not that kind of a guy.* He watched the employees enter the store in the early morning and then on other days he watched them leave. Finally, he started to stake out the parking lot across from the Jeweler as the people came and went with parcels under their arms, loading them into cars. As he surveyed the parking lot, walking from vehicle to vehicle, he tried door handles. *Wow, this guy didn't lock his car. I wonder if he does this regularly?* Day after day he kept watch on the jewelry store and the parked cars while Anita was out sight-seeing. He continued to check car doors, but the previous unlocked car was now locked. It took days of checking when he finally found another unlocked car. *Don't want to cross wires to get it started. It would take too much time. I don't want to get caught. I'm not really that gifted working with cars.* Anton looked further until he found a car with keys hanging from the side of the steering wheel. *This could be it.*

He put this car on his watch list for a few days, watching the same person come and go. Soon he knew how long that particular car stayed parked in the same place without moving.

This is the day. Anton quickly removed the key from the ignition, then cycled to the nearest auto shop to cut duplicate keys. *That was a lucky break.* He returned the key into the ignition. *It will only work if this car is parked here when I need it.*

In close proximity, while on his beat, a law enforcement officer noticed a man walking aimlessly day after day. *I might be a flic but this could prove to be interesting. I'll put him on my watch list but keep it to myself. He has to be up to something.* Allen Smart walked into the Jeweler Store where he was well known to the owner.

"Hello, Mr. Smart. How goes it out there for you?"

"Nothing happening which means you're happy, *droit*?"

"You have that right. Don't need any disturbances around here."

"By the way, Ralph, how long have you been in business here anyhow?"

The Inter Continental Carlton Cannes was a 343-room luxury hotel built in 1911 located on the French Riviera and listed by the Government of France as a National Historic Building. The hotel was a central location for the Alfred Hitchcock film *"To Catch a Thief"* starring Grace Kelly and Cary Grant. In 1970 it featured in the Peter Sellers/Goldie Hawn comedy *"There's a Girl in my Soup."* Today, however it would be the jewelry store of concern.

"My family has run this Jewelry store in this hotel for years and I'm proud to say since I've been the proprietor we've never once been robbed."

"I'll bet you're proud of that record."

"Well, you have to know, it's because of *de police* keeping an eye on my store."

"You mean the neighborhood *flic*. We try to keep an eye on everybody. Especially since you have an outside storefront and entrance. We don't always succeed but we try."

"The outside entrance gives us a better reach to people who may not necessarily lodge at the hotel. We are here for the people."

"I hardly think that's so because the gems you carry are not for the regular class of people. More for the upper class."

"Maybe, but we are here for the business clientele, then."

"You mean the international traveler, the wealthy international traveler, you might say."

"I'm glad you are on our side. We need your protection."

"Ralph, I'm planning to take a few days' holiday soon. That is, if my boss will let me get some time off."

"Who will take your place?"

"They always have guys available. You shouldn't have anything to worry about. You're in a good area and like you said nothing has happened for years, so I don't know how that would change."

Smart left and continued on his beat for the evening. *This is my district and my responsibility. That means it is all up to me. I wonder, if I can persuade my boss to send my replacement to concentrate more on the top half of my beat. I just know what this 'window shopper' is up to.*

Something I can do better in plain clothes. I don't want anyone to be aware of anything until I'm really certain.

Smart entered his precinct station finding the Police Inspector sitting behind his desk.

"Hey, Boss, what's the chance that I could have a few days off?"

"What's up, Smart? You moving or going someplace special on holiday?"

"Not sure about where I'm going to go yet. I've been saving my francs and wanted to take some time to see more of France. I get stuck in a rut these days but a day or so could do the trick."

"Go for it. Anything to report on your beat that any of us should know?"

"Seems everything is fine. Checked with the jewelry store and they seem to be doing well. Might want to keep an eye on the North end of my beat, though."

"See something suspicious there?"

"There's always something on the North side of town."

"We'll send one of our guys to take the watch for you and will relay that message."

It was all set. If he was going to watch in plain clothes, he didn't need another flic to be trailing him and he surely didn't want back up for this situation. He would keep this one to himself.

Anton continued his unrelenting venture. *Today the car he had made a key for was locked.* He gave a sigh of relief. It didn't matter now. He had a few other jobs to complete before his plan could work. *I still need another car, a car of my own. It has to be cheap.* Anton scouted about until he found a car with a *"For Sale"* sign attached to the hood. He loitered around until the owner came for his car. "For sale? Do you have the title to it?"

Smart answered, "I do. You're going to buy it?"

"If the price is right and it runs. A Renault, isn't it? I'm surprised it still runs. Can't be worth much."

"Yeah, I'm not asking much. I bought it a few years back. It runs, hear that? Purrs like a kitten."

They made the exchange. Smart asked, "It's Done. You have a driver's license, I'm sure?"

Stunned by the question, said, "I drive."

"Enjoy it."

This was only part of the plan. He drove the Renault to the pier just a few miles away timing how long it would take. Now he wanted to find a pleasure boat large enough to reach another continent. It seemed someone was always selling something but this time it had to be good enough to weather the sea farther out. There it was, another "*For Sale*" sign. *That one would certainly do but I don't know I have the money for it.*

Anton began looking around when he spotted a man sitting on the deck across from the boat of interest.

"You know who owns this rig?"

"I do."

"Interested in selling?"

"I am."

"What's the condition like?"

"Come, I'll show you around."

The owner took him below deck to show him the accommodations. "You have a complete kitchen, bed room and bathroom. Can sleep four people. I think the cupboards are still full of canned goods. I'll leave them for you if you want to buy it."

"Why would you sell it anyway? What's the engine look like?"

"Take a look. Should be enough fuel to get you to the next fuel station along the coast. I'll start it."

Engine ran smooth without a sputter. "Want to buy it?"

"I don't have a lot of money. What price you askin'?"

"Money doesn't mean so much to me. I'm getting married and my gal doesn't like the water. She wants to travel abroad, more by air."

"A cruiser?"

"Yeah, it's not a sail boat. They can be tricky to handle."

"Here's what I can give you, but I'm really sure you will want more."

The owner counted the money. "That'll do. I'll sign off the title and it's yours. Like I said, I don't need the money but I need my wife to enjoy traveling."

"Thanks. For now, I need to leave it moored here. I'll take it out tomorrow."

"That will work for now. The slip is paid for this month. After that you'll have to take care of it."

Anton sat on the boat deck for a minute with his thoughts. *I've spent a lot of money in one day and it had better pay off. The jeweler might think I'm too poor or in the wrong financial position but that won't matter.* Anton's thoughts wouldn't summarize his intent. *I just don't know if I can do this. What if Anita won't do this with me? I can't do it without her.*

Next he needed a rifle. *A rifle, the thought almost scares me but I've come this far already, I can't go back now.*

It wasn't that hard to make a fire arms purchase.

Anton saw the advertisement. "Gun show this Saturday." *Too bad I wasn't going to stay around. That might have been fun to see all the choices.* He stood looking at the selections of firearms.

"A rifle? Going hunting?"

"You might say that."

"You'll need some ammo, sir. How much?"

"I don't know the alternatives."

"Here, let me show you. We have this stuff for practice and then this kind as well."

Soon Anton was back at the Apartment but no matter how hard he tried, there was no reprieve for his restlessness. Instead, the excitement was beginning to build. The decision was made. *Now I have a key, a car and a boat. Even the method, I just have to decide the day.*

"Where were you today, Anton? I thought you were supposed to work. The boss asked if I knew where you were the last couple of days. I tried to make up an excuse so I told him you might have forgotten to call in but that you were ill today. So, what's up?"

Anita had noticed a difference in everything Anton attempted to do. He appeared aloof, almost as if he didn't notice her presence anymore.

She asked again, "Please tell me what you are up to, Anton. You're not responding to me. Do I still know you? I hope you're not into that drug stuff anymore,"

"No, Anita, I've been working on a surprise for you."

"A surprise? It's not my birthday, so what is it?"

"I want to get us to the US very soon."

"But how? Do we have enough money already? I'm sure we will never be satisfied until we do that but we are going to have to work steadier for a bit longer. You not working the last couple of days doesn't help us any. If we put our minds together and see if we can get more hours, who knows how long it will take. For the two of us, that doesn't have to take long. If this is that important to get there sooner than later,

I'll stop the sight-seeing and get another job. We just have to stop spending so much of our money."

"I don't want you to do that. My plan is better. Anita, I will give you the biggest ring money can buy."

"Are you proposing to me?"

"When I can get one of those rings for you."

"I don't really need a ring to marry you, Anton. I've been enjoying wondering about with you just the way we are. I wouldn't want to waste the money, especially if we want to get to the US soon."

"For you, it wouldn't be money wasted and it's something I have to do. I have to prove how much I love you by giving you the most. I want you to have the largest ring of all. Nothing less will do."

"I thought you said we are going to the US. How can we without any money? Anton, I don't need a ring that expensive. You could give me a wooden ring and I'd be happy."

"A good wooden ring isn't cheap either but that doesn't matter. I want a diamond ring for you and then I want to take you to the States as quickly as we can."

"We'll get there soon enough if we keep working. Maybe we need to climb some more mountains to get rid of that restlessness, you think? Get a thrill from the sights we can see."

"Oh, no you don't. I'm not sure I'd be able to rescue you a second time."

They continued eyeing the jewels in the store window while talking mostly about trivial things. Anton appeared restless, eager to complete the job he had prepared for.

"I have another proposal for us to accomplish."

"Anton, before you get involved in making proposals, I'd like to see more of France. Go from place to place together. I want you to come with me on some of my excursions because I know I still haven't seen enough. Why not, let's work a little longer here and there since that's what you like to do anyhow. Maybe that will slow us both down so we can put our plans for getting to the US together properly."

"Anita, if we keep doing that we'll never get to the US."

"Like I said, we have to somehow continue working. Any plot will have to include working for a time. How could your plan exclude working, tell me? I'd like to hear."

"We'll work all right but only for one more night."

"What are you going to do? Knock off some millionaire? Am I in this plan of yours?"

"It'll only work if you are. I need your help especially if the States is our final destination."

"Wow, hold on there. How could any scheme get us there so soon? In my mind we are going to have to keep our jobs for some time and start to earn some serious money. If you're that restless, we do need money and lots of it."

"That's what I'm talking about, Anita."

Anita ignored Anton, "I really think we need to start to sort out our lives and find the meaning of our existence or we will continue to be restless no matter what we do."

"That's exactly why I came up with a clever idea."

"You are kidding me. That's the reason for your *fantasy cloud* in the sky?"

"I'm not ready to settle down Anita, to understand our lives and find out what God has to do with it. I'm not ready for that. Just let's do this one thing and when we finally get to the States, I promise to figure life out with you."

"So then, what's so good about this imaginary way of life you keep coming up with? What will it do for us and how possibly could it get us to the States? You have to know in reality we need real money, not make believe. I mean money and the only way I know to get it is by working really hard for what we want, Anton."

"I'm not willing to do that."

"I'm afraid that maybe what you want can only lead us behind cell doors."

"Not if we do it my way."

"Nothing can possibly be fool proof."

"My idea can't fail."

Anton shared his scheme of getting rich quick with Anita.

"You want to kill everyone in sight that can identify you?"

"No killing, I promise."

"If you don't kill anyone, we'll be caught by someone who is left alive to say we did it."

Chapter Five
The Heist

They were back at their apartment now as they continued on Anton's plan he had conceived.

"I don't care what you want to do but if it means we're involved in killing, I'm not with you, I'm not touching that. No way, count me out!"

"I'm not a killer and it will never come to that, Anita."

"Then my question to you is, why do you have a machine gun in our apartment? You are telling me no one will die?"

"I promise, just follow my lead. No one will die."

"I'm just not sure about all this, Anton. Yet, you are the man that saved my life. I'll go with it."

"We have to go now, it's about quitting time, the right time."

They again cycled past the jewelry store, pushing the bikes into their stalls.

"Aren't you going to lock our bikes so they'll stay in place, Anton?"

"Why? You don't think we're going to come back for them, do you?"

"Oh."

"Just follow me." Anton hesitated as his eyes perused the parking lot carefully. "First, we have to find a particular car."

"Find a car?"

"Okay, does it sound better if I say steal a car? I've been watching the parking lot where there is a black sedan. A man parks it across the street from where I want us to be. He doesn't usually lock it but the last couple of times I checked, it was locked."

"Then how do you plan to steal it?"

"He left the keys in the ignition once so I grabbed them and had a duplicate made."

"You what?"

"We have to steal that car. When we're done we'll return it. He won't know a thing about the heist."

"So now it's a heist!"

"I checked this morning and looked again to see if that very car was parked in the same place and from my observance it stays there all day until late in the evening. For him, it isn't the normal 5 o'clock, it's more like 8 o'clock in the evening."

"You are determined to do this. Where to from there?"

"I bought an old used car, didn't register it but parked at the other end of that lot. If somehow we're followed, we'll drive a bit and then come back, park it where it belongs. Find our car and we are off. Well, you get the picture, right? Not only that, there are numerous vehicles at that time of evening for people coming and going, we won't even be noticed if we play it cool."

Anton and Anita disappeared into the dark alley between the buildings next to the Jewelry store.

"Mask up and put the disguise on."

"I'm going as a man?"

"You are and keep the gloves on, I don't want finger prints."

"Walk east and around the corner, pull our masks down and walk backwards into the store."

"Got it."

Minutes later Smart drove up with his motorcycle, stopping a quarter block back from the jewelry store, watching the front store entrance. *Must be the front entrance attendant's dinner break, he's nowhere around.* Smart continued watching. *This has to be the night. There, I see two people? Two men? I thought it would only be the one guy. I don't get it, two men? I've never seen the other person before. I wonder how that will go? They look a bit nervous, kind of fidgety and apprehensive. They'll never pull this off.* Smart watched intently, he was familiar with the reactions of the criminal mind. He had twenty years of experience and he was determined not to let this one go. Besides, this was a jewelry store. It couldn't be cash money they were after or they would have chosen a bank to rob. *Maybe they are connected to the black market?* Smart knew very well important money could be made if someone was knowledgeable. This was one feat he had never dared to accomplish for himself though he did have connections. *I think I will sneak in behind them and go in disguised, unnoticed. He has a rifle so I'll surprise them from behind. If it doesn't go well, I'll arrest them on the spot. That will make me the hero. If my plan fails, he won't get far with that Renault I sold him. It has probably only a 100 miles before it will give up. I put just enough gunk in the engine so it would have a smooth sound. He didn't know what a piece of junk he was buying from me. It'll be easy to track them down. They will be caught for the robbery. No sweat, just the plot I need.*

Smart had decided it was time to follow in behind them. He would have to be sure he wasn't seen but as soon as they would go through the door he had to be like a mime, quick motion but no words, complete silence. He had his shoes wrapped in cloth to guarantee he would not be heard.

It was nearing closing time for the Carlton Hotel Jewelry store with only a few customers still browsing around. The lights illuminated the store from within making it easy to spot how many people were still in the store and where the best surprise spot would be.

"Gloves, bandanas, socks over our heads and leave the talking to me."

"Got it Anton."

"Rifle in hand."

"Coast is clear. Do you see anyone, Anton?"

"Nobody, just a few people in the store."

The Hotel was an elaborate historical building with domes on the seaward corners. Considered a luxury hotel, the place to stay. Active with patrons coming and going but at dinnertime there was usually a definite pause, no one seemed to come in or go out for about ten minutes. Every day that Anton had watched without fail the outside attendant for the Hotel would take a break from his duty. This would clear the way for their surprise entrance. They could go in unnoticed. "Three minutes is all we need, Anita."

"I'm sure. Can't be longer for this to work."

Within seconds the two entered.

"Get down, all of you!" Immediately Anton sprayed his machine gun fire. Customers and employees panicked, huddling in terror. "Get down, or be shot!" People were afraid that they could be the next to die, as bullets could be heard everywhere, crisscrossing the room.

Then in total disbelief Anton stood dazed when he saw a masked man standing between him and Anita with an open satchel. No words, no one made a sound. He couldn't afford to botch this, they had to go with the change in events. No one made a sound. All Anton could do was sweep jewels in both cases hoping it would work. The stranger wouldn't be satisfied. Without the use of spoken words, he motioned he wanted more. Anton saw him reach in his side pocket for what he knew would be a revolver.

Anton felt his blood boil. He turned to point his rifle at him. The stranger closed his satchel and disappeared out the door.

On the way out, Anita emptied the cash drawer, stuffing the proceeds in her side pouch. If nothing else, at least they had some cash. After all, that's all that she wanted.

Anton and Anita ran out the back entrance, ripped off their disguise and ditched them in a trash barrel.

"We have to walk out of here with intent, with purpose. Head east and around the corner."

"Got it."

"Put the jewels in the backpack, stuff the empty satchel under the car. When we drive away, that satchel will be on the ground, empty."

"Why not throw it in the dumpster?"

"If someone wants to follow us, it'll be a distraction. They will want to see what's in it. Get in the car, Anita!"

They drove the stolen car back to its original spot.

"They're onto us, Anton. You can hear the sirens."

"They're busy at the store, see?" It appeared as if every cop car from the neighborhood was now surrounding the jewelry store.

"Walk casually."

"I'm following you. Where is your car?"

"See, in the corner? It's the Renault, the orange and white car."

"Wow, if someone knows, we are a dead give-a-way."

Smart was now outside the store, standing beside his motorcycle. He had stuffed his disguise in his bikes side pocket, then waited for the other two to come out of the store. *I don't get it? I can't see the Renault anywhere. I was sure he was the guy I sold the car to. The car won't go very far. I have a good idea where he lives, I've watched him enough times cycling to his apartment. The car has to be here somewhere. I want to catch him with the stolen jewels and arrest him for the heist.* Smart drove his motorcycle in and out of the parking lot looking again until he spotted the Renault at a distance. *A man and a woman, not the two men in the jewelry heist. I don't get it. I'll watch to see if they are going toward the car.* He waited. *Just as I thought, they are heading in that direction.*

"We are being followed Anton. Let's just walk normally to the car."

"Don't look now but you are about to meet the man I bought this Renault from. He's on that motorcycle behind us."

"What does he want? You paid him, didn't you?"

"I did."

"The satchel, Anton, he has that satchel, can you see it? He has to be that same guy."

"Walk normal, he doesn't expect a woman, remember?"

"Look, he got off the motorcycle."

Smart's steps became swifter.

Anton and Anita could almost feel Smart breathing. He was too close. "Hey, guys, why in such a hurry?"

Anton turned to look. "Didn't realize it was you."

"Still like the car?"

"It seems fine to me. Thanks for selling it to me."

"I know a good place to have dinner."

"I think we'll pass on that offer. Sorry, we're a bit busy. We have a meeting in town and we're almost late."

"You don't look like business people."

Anton stiffened up. "I don't look the part, eh?"

"Please, Anton." Anita nudged him, she needed to bring him into reality.

"What part of town is the meeting in?"

"It's just around the corner from the car dealership in midtown. Maybe we can talk some other time."

Smart lingered as he watched the car sputter. *I'll just keep a close eye on them and just maybe I can get involved in helping with the car.*

"We're dead, Anton."

"Be patient. It started before and it will start now." Finally, the engine sputtered to life as they started out. "I'm going to have to make it look like I'm going toward midtown."

"I have news for you, Anton, he's following us which means we have to go to midtown."

"Maybe I can pretend to park it in that multistory parking garage. Pay the parking fee so he'll believe we are going to a meeting."

"When we see him do the same, we'll leave."

"How dare him assume I don't look the part of a business person."

"Let it go, we don't have the time to confront him."

It wasn't long before Anton and Anita drove into the parking structure while they watched. Smart took the bait. While Smart was busy parking his motorcycle, Anton quickly drove out. The parking attendant began a conversation, "Oh, you didn't stay? There is no fee when you leave so quickly. You haven't clocked any time. Let me clear the ticket."

"Please can we just go? We're being followed, our lives are in danger."

"Just take a minute. You said your lives are in danger? Here, I'll call the police."

"Don't do that. I don't want you to call the police, I can't wait for them."

"Who is following you?"

"It's the guy on the motorcycle."

"I have to call the cops, but I'll lift bars to let you out."

They sped down the ramp and around the corner.

"I need to take the long way around so that Smart doesn't follow."

The parking attendant stopped the speeding motorcycle. "You can't go through, man. I've just called the cops on you."

"Sir, I am the police, I'm after that Renault." Smart flashed his badge.

"Oh, I'm sorry."

Those blasted guys split out on me but I know that car can't go far. I'll find them. Smart was bewildered as his eyes searched everywhere. *How'd they do that?* Smart drove around several blocks hoping the car would have stalled out and then he'd see them somewhere. *Where they live is where I'll find them, that's it. I have a good idea where his neighborhood was. The Renault will be parked at his apartment.*

Smart sped past the police station. Soon the sirens began to follow him. *Oh, blast that lot attendant. Now I've done it. I'll have to share the glory of the apprehension of those guys.*

Smart stopped his motorcycle for the approaching officer. "Smart! I thought you were on holiday? Why are you speeding out here? I'm the guy that's assigned to your beat."

"I thought I saw the jewelry heist suspect and I didn't want to lose him."

"You spotted the get-a-way car?"

"Yeah, it's a Renault."

"I thought you drove a Renault."

"I did. It wasn't running too well so I sold it."

"You feisty old buzzard, you probably sold it for more than it was worth."

"Made a few bucks."

"Okay, let's find this guy you were following." Smart parked his motor cycle and drove off with Nichols. "Where to, Smart?"

They quickly sped to the neighborhood perceived to be Anton's home.

"This is the apartment building but I don't know which one he lived in."

"Let's go ask. The managers usually live on the bottom floor."

They knocked and the door opened. They gave the description of Anton. "We saw him with a man and then another girl."

"I rented the room to Anton and Anita. No one else is allowed to live here with them."

Smart inquired, "Are they here?"

"No, they took all their belongings and left. Didn't even stay to the end of the month."

"Where did they say they were going?"

"The lady said, *far away.* I asked what that meant. They wouldn't tell me. Are they wanted by the law? They were my best tenants."

"Where did they work?"

"I don't ask and they never told me. All I wanted was the rent money. The rest isn't my business."

"How about some of the other people living here?"

"Knock and ask."

They did that. A little girl answered the door. Smart asked, "Little lady, did you know your neighbors here?"

"Anita? She was a nice lady. Want to see what she gave me?" The little girl ran back into the apartment to find her toy when her mother appeared. "What do you want of my daughter, she hasn't done anything."

"We are asking about your neighbor. Is it Anton and Anita? Did you know them? Did they say where they were going?"

"Don't know anyone and please don't bother us. I have a sick husband to take care of." She slammed the door.

"I don't know what to say Smart."

"Sorry Nichols, I thought I had them."

"Tell me, how did you think they would be a suspect?"

Smart fumbled with words. He couldn't say he had robbed the jewelry store along with them, nor could he say he had seen the man check out the jewelry store several times. Asking his boss for the time off and then didn't report the suspect? In fact, he had reported all was well in this neighborhood. Smart had to think fast. "When I heard the sirens go off at the jewelry store, instead of joining everyone there, I went looking for who could have done this."

"But, Smart, you were supposed to be gone on holiday, remember?"

"Oh that, I was on my way out of town when I heard the noise as I passed by here."

"In the middle of your vacation and this isn't even near where you live?"

Smart had to change the scene as quickly as possible. "Drive around the jewelry store. Maybe we can spot something." They drove around to the back of the hotel. "Look what I see, a satchel?"

"Tell me Smart, why is that satchel important?"

"Think about it Nichols, that's almost brand new. Open it."

"I don't get it, Smart, nothing in it. Empty. I saw you have one just like it. Let's look in yours."

"Can't let you do that."

"Oh yeah?" Nichols wasn't that naive, he knew the score. "Half?"

"Quickly, let's get in the boat. Give me your hand, Anita. Are you in?"

"I am."

The Bay was peaceful, blue smooth water. "Feels so nice. How far are we planning on going today, Anton?"

"See where the night takes us."

"Anton, can you see the Dolphins? They're all around us, like everywhere."

"Look! Did you see the whale, Anita?"

"I did. It almost looks like the Dolphins are trying to tell us something."

Anton was more interested in the successful heist. "This day couldn't be better. The water and atmosphere is clear everywhere you look."

The Bay of Biscay is located off the North coast of Spain and the West coast of France in the Atlantic Ocean south of the Celtic Sea. It is known for its severe winter storms. There are at least 200 varieties of fish in the bay with many Dolphin and Whale sightings.

"Aren't the waves getting too rough for this little cruiser?"

"Didn't expect that. Just minutes ago it was as smooth as glass. Now a storm is brewing? We have no choice but to go with it, Anita, we can't turn back. Got to do it."

Anton continued racing the cruiser through the rugged waves as the wind blew unceasingly.

Often without warning the Bay of Biscay can have some of the fiercest weather conditions during the winter months. The huge pressure differences cause stronger westerly winds and longer waves. Historians have detailed hundreds of shipwrecks and lost lives. In recent history the number of shipwrecks have declined because of the forecasting system in place. However, Anton and Anita were not in tune with weather forecasting but more with how they could eventually make it to the Americas. Winter was now officially in full swing. Anton and Anita started off for places yet unknown, in their Cabin Cruiser with some confidence.

"Got enough of the jewels, Anton? Whose speedboat is this anyhow?"

"I bought it from the owner at the dock."

"You had the money for this?"

"It didn't cost a lot, the owner just wanted to unload it for what I could offer."

"You spent every last cent we had."

"The owner gave me the title signed off and I gave him what I had."

"I guess that was clever and you didn't register it either. Have to hand it to you, almost like you've done this before. The guy's car you used is where it was in the first place, so he wouldn't be any wiser unless he wrote down the miles on the speedometer. Unlikely he'd do that because everything was left as it was. Besides, it wasn't driven but a couple city blocks, if that. But I have to ask you, the other guy that followed us in the jewelry store, how did he know we were about to rob it?"

"That was a little frightening."

"I'll bet he's been watching you. You might have appeared somewhat suspicious?"

"How would he know what I was up to? I even used a disguise."

"A disguise?"

"Well, I used different hats and jackets every day."

"You call that a disguise, Anton? I have a suspicion he saw someone at the store too often. Just think, if he is a *flic* or a cop and that's his beat, aha, there you have it."

"When I was looking for cars, Smart happened to be there."

"He was there by no accident. He had it all planned. Get in on the heist and blame you. If he really is a cop he'd be able to find your name in the transfer of title."

"He might have been hoping for that but we didn't discuss names."

"What Smart didn't plan on was our car switch. He wanted you to use the Renault."

"I don't get it. If he is a cop, why didn't he arrest me?"

"The jewels bought him. He wanted part of the stash and then let you take the rap for the heist. Smart is true to his name."

"But, Anita, he has to catch us with the goods. We dumped the satchel for him to find. What might have added to the confusion was that there is no longer two men. He found us as a couple, so he's still not sure."

"The thing that bothers me, Anton, he gets in on the heist, robs the store with us and then when we go to dinner with him, he'll find a way to search us so that he can make the arrest. We take the rap. How cruel is that? He isn't even an honest cop."

"Yeah, Anita, who are we to report him? We aren't innocent, so we can't do that even if we wanted to."

"Oh but we could."

"How do you figure, Anita?"

"Give the jewelry back, report him. He gets searched and he goes to jail."

"Not so fast, we started this heist, we'd get time for what we planned."

"We'd have a clean conscience."

"But, we would never reach the Americas, especially with a record against our names. Never again wander the globe. Don't think I can do that."

"If we ever get caught, Smart makes a name for himself and we're done, Anton."

"Not likely because we are on our way to *nowhere*."

"He almost had us. Imagine following us to the parking yard. That was close. It's a good thing we never gave anyone information about who we are. He's got to be trying to find us even now."

"He isn't interested in catching us and if he is, we are nowhere to be found. No, he's busy spending his jewels by now."

"I saw you point your rifle at him. Anton, you were going to shoot him and you promised there would be no killing."

"I didn't kill him, did I?"

Anita had a hard time letting it go. "I can't believe that. You sprayed the Jeweler store with fire power. Not only that, we might have been caught red handed. No more schemes please, Anton. While you two were going after the jewels, I emptied the cash register. I figured we needed paper money more than the jewels. I'm really angry with you because you promised there would be no killing and how many people died in this heist?"

"Let me show you." Anton pointed his machine gun at the bottom of the boat.

"Anton what are you doing? You are crazy, you want to kill us both?"

He started shooting. "Look, we aren't sinking."

"What are you using for ammunition?"

Chapter Six
The Storm Rages On

The raging wind continued in strength and it didn't appear it would let up any time soon. Anton attempted to steer the cruiser to keep it afloat as it rocked back and forth. It took all he had in energy struggling every minute to steady it.

"It feels like we are in a bowl of jelly, like we could capsize any time. How many knots do you think this wind is blowing?"

"It's bad."

"If we hit the rocks, we're done. All the jewels in the world won't help us. I'm praying we will get somewhere safe soon."

"Praying? Since when did you start to pray, Anita?"

"As a kid, I'd pray when I got myself into trouble and somehow God always got me through everything. I prayed on the mountain when I realized I was alone and was about to die when you came and rescued me."

"I don't think that God would have anything to do with us. What we did was absolutely wrong. How is God supposed to help us when we did the wrong thing? I think, Anita, we have to go this one on our own. I'm not giving myself up. Are you going to turn yourself over to the law?"

Anita didn't answer. She had never thought about that before. She thought that no matter what, God was there to help her. This time she was clearly not doing what God would have wanted for her. This couldn't be good.

"I'm sorry, Anita for disrupting your thoughts."

Anita was silent and then asked, "When you bought this rig, did you think to store any food in it?"

"It came with food. Probably enough to last us for a bit. I've never been in this bay before so I don't know how long this storm will last."

"If we find land on time, it will be the least we could hope for."

"What, you aren't praying?"

"Like you said, you don't want us to turn ourselves over to the authorities. After all, that's what God would demand, don't you think?"

Anton wasn't about to add to the discussion, "I had better turn off the engines before we use up all our fuel. Can't fight this one, we'll have to wait it out. We may be fortunate and only experience the perimeter of the storm. If that's the case, we could survive."

"You're thinking there is a chance we won't?"

"Who knows," he hesitated, "but we'll give it all we have. It would be smart to keep our life jackets on."

"Anton, you realize if someone finds us alive, we have to dump the jewels, right?"

"I guess."

"We did this, why?"

"So we could get to the Americas."

The hurricane raged on for an eternity or so it seemed. Anita was convinced they were feeling the effects from the center of the storm but as Anton said, they were probably only experiencing the whiplash from the wind on the outer edges.

In the Bay of Biscay weather can turn severe often without warning. As the season approaches winter, depressions tend to form in the West, eventually appearing to die out. Yet, as quickly as they disappear they tend to reform into thunderstorms. That brings the constant rain into the area with what looks like crashing hurricanes in the bay. Merchant seamen fear the severity, as container ships have lost their cargo in the bay along with many lives.

Anton and Anita clung to their life jackets as the wind continued to howl tossing them back and forth. They feared that going below deck to relax and should the cruiser capsize, there would be no chance of survival so they stayed in the cockpit towards the aft. It was all they could do with the force of the wind. The torrential rain continued. Finally, after hours of the boat being tossed around, it started to feel more like rain than gale forces.

"I'm tired, Anton. This has been too much for me and I've completely lost track of the days we've been pushed about in the sea."

"Why don't you sleep for a while? I think we are under control for now."

"I'll crash just where I am."

"Too afraid, Anita?"

Anita didn't answer, sleep overtook her as she stretched out on the leather like, waterproof upholstered seats.

It seemed like days that they had been tossed about when it became apparent they would have to ration their food supply. Sharing what food and fresh water they still had, Anton began to show concern but Anita felt it better not to make any comments.

Then somehow from nowhere, the storm began to pass over as the boat began to bob up and down, floating. "Do we have enough gas to get anywhere or are we just in the center of the storm where it is supposed to be quiet, Anton?"

Using the binoculars, Anton perused the water to see if he could get a glimpse of land somewhere. "Look, Anita, the sun! The clouds just parted."

"We made it!"

"We did, but to where?" Anton started the engine up. It sputtered and spat. He tried again, but it had gotten too wet. "We'll have to drift for a bit until we dry out."

"Maybe we'll drift closer to land."

It could have been a few hours or even a day of sleeping. It was as if their bodies felt nothing anymore. They were tired from the tossing about in the Cabin Cruiser. Anita awoke with a start, "Where are we, Anton?" Looking about, "Look, the land is close!"

Anton tried desperately to open his eyes. "We are where, did you say?"

"Check your charts, maybe we can tell."

Anton and Anita checked and re checked the maps. "Okay, let's see if we can make it to shore. Maybe the water is shallow enough for us to wade in."

"Anton, look, have you noticed?"

"What?"

"We're starting to take on water. Can we plug the holes?"

"Must've hit some rocks. At least we made it out of the country, hopefully we will avoid a prison term." Anton seemed concerned.

"That means we have to be where?"

"Do you still have the jewels?"

"I do, we still have the backpack." Anita opened it as the jewels shimmered in the sunlight. "Okay, I'm sure we have enough of the jewels for us." She zipped it up. "Why don't we just travel? No one knows who we are if we just keep going about. Besides they will be looking for three people, remember there were three people that robbed the jewelry store."

"We can't do a lot until we try to unload the gems." Anton knew this wasn't going to be easy.

"We have to find a way to put them into cash, don't you think? How do we do that without getting caught?"

"Find the black market."

"We'll never get full value."

"We barter, Anita."

"While someone holds a gun to our heads, is that what you want?"

"Let's just get to shore. Looks like a good beach, should be able to walk to somewhere. Let's go, we've taken on too much water, we need to get going."

"For your information, Anton, I don't swim. Wading won't do for me but if we can walk in, I can hold onto you and I'll be fine."

"You can't swim? I'll have to rescue you one more time?" Anton made a jump into the water. "I can stand, so come, Anita, take my hand and hang onto me. Let's try."

"Just like I thought, Anton, you got us marooned on a deserted island. None of these jewels will do us any good."

"Settle down, Anita. Look past the sand on this beach. See the trees? Then look again, there are buildings. Can you see them?"

"We'll wonder around when we reach the shore and you will be surprised what we can find. Hang on to me and keep your life jacket on."

"Shouldn't we pull the boat to shore with us and repair it so that we can use it again?"

"Too big for us to pull in and it would be better to let it go. Should anyone have seen us leave in the boat, we will be considered missing and dead. It's going to sink anyhow."

"Could we puncture more holes in the bottom to help it sink faster with your machine gun? Do you have any real ammunition?"

"No, I don't. Just let's leave it alone. Another storm will take care of its demise. With any luck it will eventually capsize."

"We can only hope."

"No praying?"

"You are making fun of me now. Someday, you will know."

Anita hung on to Anton as she had been instructed. As difficult as it was, they walked through the water with their backpacks.

"Hopefully, we will find people who don't speak our native tongue. Then we'll know we made it to somewhere far away."

Chapter Seven
Pay The Fine

"What's the plea?"

It was a Monday morning in the City of Los Angeles with Judge Pride residing to hear the case of a Cost Accountant Verses Traverse Trucking Company.

"Your Honor, I am not guilty on the grounds that someone else tampered with the books. I can prove it. Not even the hand writing corrections are mine."

The judged ignored the plea, "You can pay the $5000 fine or spend a year in jail and ask for a retrial."

"I don't have $5000, Sir."

Someone from the courtroom stood up. "Your Honor, I will pay his fine if you release him to my custody."

The anvil fell to the desk. "Settled. Pay the fine to the bailiff and you are free to go."

It was over but Bill was bewildered. How did this happen? That meant he was guilty and he didn't even have a chance for a fair trial. Wasn't he supposed to have the right for an assigned Attorney? What was happening? Oh, he had known for some time that someone in the company had been tampering with his entries in the books. At first he hesitated saying anything. He came in early enough each day so that he could correct the books as they should be. Quitting the job was not an option, he couldn't afford to be without employment. He desperately needed that paycheck he depended on. Finally, he reported it to the owners of the company and then this happened. He couldn't believe what he was hearing and then someone was now going to pay his fine?

A men stood outside the courtroom waiting for him. "What just happened? Who are you anyhow?"

"I just paid your fine, Bill. My name is George."

"Why?"

"I want you to come work for me."

"But I'm not guilty and I can prove it. I just need a lawyer."

"Awe, don't worry about them. I know all about that judge, he regularly gets paid off for the decision he makes. Someone would have had to ask for the decision he gave you. As long as he can be out on the golf course on his designated times he's happy. You should see the mansion that guy lives in."

"How would you know about that judge?"

"I have connections and that's why I'm offering you a job in my company."

"I'm not sure I want to work for you or anyone else before I clear my good name."

"Have it your way. I know for a fact that judge fills his pockets all the time. He just hasn't gotten caught yet. I'm offering you a job because I need an honest man like you."

"What kind of work are you in?"

"I just merely want you to honestly handle the books for my company. Money will come in and then you will have bills I give you to pay. That's all there is to it. It has to be all done legally. I perceive you to be honest especially as I listen to you. I can't afford to have the IRS audit our books and if they do, you need to be able to handle that."

"You're paying what?"

"Plenty and more than you were making before. I'm a very fair man, you'll see."

"Suppose I don't have any other choice."

"Good, then it's settled."

"When and where do I start?"

George took him to a place he called his office.

That wasn't his first deal he made to have someone join his employment. In fact, there were others but George had been spying out the land with a plan to put together a team of men to join in his business venture when he spotted a drug deal go down. Today, he wasn't so interested in the drug pushers that had just been arrested by the cops swarming the park. Instead, his eyes were focused on the park bench where he watched a homeless man with nothing to do, minding his own business.

"Hey man, did you see what I saw?"

"I did."

"And you are part of that aren't you? I'm going to call the authorities and have you arrested."

"I wasn't part of it and you know it."

"Well, here's a choice. I won't say anything but I want you to be my sidekick."

"Your what?"

"You know, just be there with me on my rounds."

"What, you into pushing drugs?"

"You watch my back and I watch yours."

"What's in it for me?"

"Money."

"Start talking."

"You will have to dress like a respectable man. Lighten up on the drinking. No drinking on the job and that means around me unless I offer it to you."

"I can give it a try."

"This is for keeps, man. My name is George. You are?"

"Sam."

"Come with me, let's get you dressed. Follow me to my office."

Sam hesitated.

"Want me to call the cops?"

"You don't have anything on me."

"I could surprise you."

"You're a rotten conniver."

"Call me a con man if you like, but come with me. The money is good working for me."

They entered a little corner storefront. "Bill. I want you to meet my bodyguard."

Bill looked up from his work, "Okay."

"This is Bill. Sam and I are going to do some clothes shopping and then we'll be back. Keep the office running. Were you able to find everything you need, Bill?"

"Still looking for your books."

"It's a new business, a start-up. Here is a couple of bucks. Why don't you go to the nearest stationery store and buy whatever you need and put this office in order? Is $1000 enough?"

"If it doesn't include my salary."

"It doesn't."

"Going to need furnishings, too, you know. That will be a lot more."

"Whatever, do whatever you must to make this a respectable office and I'll pay."

Bit by bit George was putting his team together. Each one he employed he had done a favor for or so he had them believe.

"How do I look?"

"Debonair, you look good and you dress better than I do. That's what I like but I just need you to watch my back. Like I said, you're my bodyguard. If you see anything that is out of place I need you to say so. I will test you from time to time. I have to be sure you are alert."

"What's the pay like?"

"The pay is you get what you want, as long as I don't want it. Sometimes we are called to go to parties and you will enjoy those as well but remember you are foremost my bodyguard. Tomorrow we go to a rifle range."

"I'm not a killer. I don't mind showing you how good I am but I refuse to do any killing. I might have to rethink this."

"Too late buddy. You won't have to shoot anyone but you need to be armed in case someone wants to take me out."

"I'm not sure about any of this."

"Too late if you don't want to be rubbed out. You got it?"

"I hear you."

It had been a few weeks since George had managed to deceitfully influence his team together. Today, he was about to get itchy feet, he needed to generate income followers. His pushers needed the stuff which meant he needed to find a lucrative way to satisfy his suppliers and that meant he needed the supplies.

"Guys, we're going to Mexico City. We need to drum up business and I think that's the place to do it. Want to come, Bill?"

"I think I'd better stay here to pay bills and take care of the home front."

"Okay, Bill. That sounds reasonable. Then it's just you and me, Sam."

"Sounds like fun. Maybe I can find myself a Seniority."
"Could be good for business, let's do it."
"Driving or flying?"
"Ah, let's pay the bucks and fly. Bill you arrange that and a place to stay. We'll be back in an hour and ready to go."
Cheaper if you wait a couple of weeks before you have to fly."
"When I say we go, we go. Get us the tickets for tonight."
"Done."

Sam was beginning to think he had made a good deal, after all. Traveling to Mexico? Why not? *Just maybe I won't come back. Wouldn't that be a blast?*

"I'll need a couple of bucks, George. How about it?"
"Leave the spending to me. Anything you want, just ask me."
He might want it that way, but I know how to hustle, I'll find my way around.

Off they were to the local pub to discuss plans between George and Sam.

Chapter Eight
Spain

———

"I can't go much further, Anton, I'm really tired."
It was a struggle walking through the sand after the arduous task of surviving the storm in the boat.
"*Posada*? Let's go there, I don't care what the hotel looks like."
They slept the night and day away when Anita awoke with a jerk. "What's going on?"
"I thought I'd let you sleep for a bit. I found some food for us to eat."
"You scared me Anton. Didn't know where I was for a minute."
"There's nothing but cold water, Anita. I showered anyhow but I don't know if you can."
Anton and Anita had finished what food they had, "If you are up to it, Anita, let's see what we can talk ourselves into."
Walking the dusty walkway past the stores, it didn't appear deserted. There was a bar and a spattering of stores scattered about. People were milling about everywhere shopping in the local stores. Anton and Anita passed by the street corner entertainment. A violin player in front of a store, then a few blocks down the road a guitarist playing next to an empty sombrero. It appeared the man with the sombrero had collected a few coins already. *Mendigos* everywhere selling wares, running up and down the sidewalks with the hope someone would buy their hand made trinkets.
"Need to find a bank."

"You can count me out, I'm not getting into robbing banks. I'm not doing any more of that stuff, Anton. What we did was hard enough. I don't think I should've been a part of that."

"No, I mean we have to exchange our money, or at least the money you got from the *cash drawer,* remember? Then start to nose around to see what we can find. This town can't be that innocent."

"What, find some drunk people in a bar and see what they have to say?"

"Why didn't I think of that, thanks, Anita."

Anita pulled Anton close. "Let's walk beside the beach. I love to watch the waves come in. Right now it is so peaceful, not at all like that fierce storm we were driven into, it changed so quickly. We were very lucky that boat didn't take on water when we were out in the middle of nowhere, Anton."

Anita knew full well it was God that had saved them even if they had done wrong. God was still showing them mercy, there was a chance. They could listen but she knew that Anton wasn't about to.

Anton could read Anita only too well but he wasn't about to give in to her thinking. "It certainly has changed. We could have gotten farther if we hadn't been so battered. That cruiser couldn't have taken much more."

"Not a lot of homes on the shoreline, Anton, or maybe they are just a bit inland."

"I can see some adobe buildings a little way up the hill."

"There's a bank. Isn't that a bank? It says, *casa de banca.* That's right, they do speak Spanish."

"I thought you knew that from the name of the hotel."

"I guess I did but to someone as tired as me? That means we only got as far as Spain. We spent all that time on the water and get marooned only to find out we are in Spain?"

Anton began to realize, "If we unload the money here, the authorities follow the trail. Jewels aren't that easy to get rid of this close to the source. Can't stay around."

"Let's hide the jewels and check everything out for now. Don't try to sell them here but check out the lay of the land."

"Check out the lay of the land? Anita, I like that. Let's do it. Or we take the money we have and take a flight to Mexico City and then work our way up to the US border. It will be a better place to unload the jewels. It will be much easier."

"I'd rather keep the jewels hidden. Check things out here for a while. If the jewels don't show up anywhere they'll forget it ever happened."

"I wouldn't worry about that. The insurance company will have paid the losses so they'll stop looking. That means we can go to Mexico City anytime we want."

"Anton, any suggestions on hiding the jewels?"

"Sew them in our clothes."

"They will get a bit heavy."

"Let's figure this out while we sit on the beach. Besides, Anita, I need some *weed*."

"Just when did you start smoking that stuff again? I thought you were clean."

"I've always done it from time to time. I need some now."

"Who's going to sell it to you?"

"I think I know where."

While Anita lay on the beach resting, Anton walked through the sand a little to the West. Soon he was back smoking his weed.

"Who gave you that?"

"I bought it."

"With what Anton?"

"I gave him a couple of stones."

"You what?" Anita jumped up. "We need to get out of here."

"Why?"

"Now someone knows what we are carrying. I'm out of here with you or without you." Anita was up on her feet, gathering her belongings.

"Where are you going?"

"You wanted to get to Mexico City. Well, I'm on my way to find the airport, no more loitering, Anton."

"Let me finish what I have."

"I'm leaving. I refuse to wait for anyone. Either you're coming with me or you're staying. I'm going and I'm going now."

"Anita! Nothing's going to go wrong."

"I'm not waiting to find out. Are you coming?"

Anton relented and joined Anita. "Okay, let's catch a cab to the airport."

"Cost too much money. I saw a bus, let's board that."

"Oh, whatever, I still don't know what the panic is about."

"If you don't think we should be in a panic, just look down the beach from where you were. How many guys would you say are coming toward us? On second thought, let's grab that cab and let's get out of here, now."

The two of them hailed a cab, "Where to?"

It was easy to hear that Anita was in a panic, "We want to get to the Airport and we need you to lose those guys in that black car. Can you do that?"

"Watch me!" It seemed the cab driver loved high-speed chases and he was about to give the black car a chase. The cab driver went in and out of traffic as though he had done many times before. "I have an idea, guys. See that store? I'll let you out in front of it. There's a back exit, I'll be waiting for you."

The black car wasn't far behind. Anton and Anita darted into the clothing store behind clothing racks. "There's a stall. Let's hide in there."

"Get out of here!" A lady who was trying on cloths gave out a scream.

Anton and Anita began posing as manikins. It seemed the men were about to give up the chase when they turned to look again. Anton and Anita stopped and stood stone still in a pose. When it didn't seem as though they were pursued any further they left through the store's back exit.

To their relief, the cab was still waiting. "You made it!"

"We made it by the skin of our teeth."

"I'll have you at the airport in a few minutes."

The cab driver was true to his word. Anton was about to pay the fare when Anita shoved him aside and gave him the pesos from her purse. She tipped him well for getting them out of their plight.

"Be better if we get as far away as we can from here. No time to loiter, Anton."

Chapter Nine
Mexico City

"Which airport do we fly into, Anton?"

"I guess with over 1,800 airports in Mexico, it does make choosing the right one a bit tricky. Almost as easy as flipping a coin to choose the best for us."

They were sitting in the terminal waiting to board their flight to Mexico City.

"I don't think you are allowed to smoke here, what are you doing, Anton?"

"I'm not going to smoke the stuff."

"Is that snuff?"

"You could say that."

Law enforcement with machine guns appeared everywhere with dog sniffing patrol.

"What's that all about, Anita? Look at all the police in the terminal. Someone is already being hand cuffed?"

"I can't believe this! They are the same guys that were after us, don't you think? I thought we lost them."

"Don't have to worry about them, see that? The cops have taken them away."

"Anton, they aren't done yet. Now they're coming our way. I'll bet they told them we might be here and they think they can find us with the dog sniffers. You didn't bring that stuff with you, did you?"

"That weed cost me too much."

"The Cops are after us."

"Don't sweat it. It's all hidden in one of those camera protection bags. It should be safe because of the lining. Besides, I paid good money."

"Problem is you paid with diamonds! That's why we've been in so much trouble already. What if they ask you to open your backpack? You better pray they don't!"

"What good is praying when I'm doing what is against the law?"

"Maybe God will help me. You fool! Get rid of those drugs right now or I don't even want to know you. Dogs can smell through anything! What a fool I am for not knowing you would bring it all with you. Taking it with you is just stupid, what'd you think they train those dogs for."

Anton grabbed his bag with the drugs, dumped it into the nearest trash bin. Both of them walked to a food stand for a cappuccino. "They'll not find anything on us."

"Look, the dogs are at that trash bin already. If someone saw you, we are done."

"Doesn't seem anyone cared to recognize us."

"You want to thank God for that."

"Sorry Anita, God wasn't in on that plan."

"He has more to do with it than you may think. Anton, please don't do that again when I'm with you. Stupid people inevitably get caught. They're still looking for someone else and it better not be us."

It was a close call but fortunate for them, the flight went without incident. Anton might have had no more drugs but they were both loaded with diamonds.

"You know Anton, it's a good job they don't inspect us bodily. I'm surprised that by now, 1994, they would, lucky for us they don't."

"They do if they get suspicious, but then how would they know. Those guys that were chasing us didn't get a good look and the cops would have thought the dogs could find the drugs. So they did."

"Fortunate for you, the trash bin was handy."

Anton and Anita slept through most of the flight time. Too tired to care about anything.

They arrived at Mexico International Airport, tired and hungry. It became a tiring task finding a hotel that would have to become the scouting point for underground jewel buyers.

"I must say, Anton, this isn't the kind of traveling I had in mind. When we originally met, we had the dream to travel carefree. This doesn't fit that bill anymore."

"Don't go soft on me now. It will take the two of us to get through this."

"Worth the cost?"

"Think about it, Anita. We'll be millionaires. Is that so bad? We'll get to the United States, buy a home and have children. Have whatever you want."

"And in hiding the rest of our lives. Get rich quick isn't much fun after all."

"I promise it won't always be like this. Help me make inquiries. Like I said, we'll find a local bar. Treat some people to a little booze and see if they will talk."

"You're going to have to get somebody really drunk for what you want to do. I would like to get rid of the jewels but you have to admit that could get a bit tricky. We should have taken the watches, rings and that kind of stuff instead of just diamonds."

"It wouldn't be as easily unloaded. Those they'd detect if we tried to unload them. Underground jewel traders want jewels. They can make them into jewelry and get away with selling that stuff in their stores. Too bad we can't do that."

"No more plans and schemes."

It wasn't long before townspeople's curiosity took hold. Blonde gal and both fair skinned, the two of them stood out among the dark skinned Mexicans. The sun tended to give Mexican blondes a bronze look. Anton and Anita were obviously from the North. People listened to these two strangers as Anton started making inquiries, "Hey, any of you guys do any gold digging anymore?"

"Got to be kidding. That hasn't happened for years. Nothing here but dry sand. Dust, I meant dust."

"Come on guys, don't let these people think we have nothing but dust and sand. Look at all the Cacti, the blossoms they give us. We have trees everywhere. Native to our climate, *Bird of Paradise* plants that give us red and yellow flowers. Let's not belittle our wonderful climate."

Anita asked, "Is that why you live here?"

"That's why I live here."

"Jim? He lives up in the hills where it isn't so hot. He has the money. That's why he lives here."

"If you guys wanted to work for a living like I do you could buy or build a home up in the mountains. Taking a few too many siestas, is your problem." The bar tender knew what he was talking about.

The jeering came. Light skinned fools, as they were called. They were green behind the ears, knowing nothing about the Mexican way of life.

"I dare you to eat our food."

Anton insisted, "It can't be that bad. I've eaten hot food before."

Soon the bar was full of laughter and more jeers.

"Here, let me order you a plate of our favorite food. Give these people a plate of the hottest peppers you have and I dare them to eat it."

"You go ahead Anton. If you can take it, I'll try. Otherwise, no thanks." Anita was no fool. She wasn't about to handle something without knowing how Anton would fair.

Anton tasted but he immediately realized he needed to accept defeat. "Sorry guys. You have me there."

The two of them continued on to yet another bar in the Mexican Desert. Anton made more inquiries and to his surprise, he wasn't hearing about the underground jewel dealers but he was hearing about money making ideas.

"Don't kid these people, Sam. We have a lot going on here. If you know the right people you can carry drugs across the US border and get paid plenty." It seemed this was no secret but then they were miles away from that crossing. However, Sam had sparked Anton's interest now. He was listening.

"Oh George, these people aren't interested in stuff like that. Blonde Europeans are too easily spotted. You are from Europe?"

Anton ignored the question but asked, "And you know people who do that and get away with it?"

"George always thinks he has connections." Sam knew only too well what the score was for them.

"In fact, when there's a sand storm brewing, it means visibility will be zero. I hear that's when everyone who wants to become wealthy makes a run across the line. However, there is only one problem."

"What's the problem, George?"

"After you make your sale, you have to wait until the storm brews up again to come back. You can't always make it back resulting in most of the guys getting caught for being in the States illegally."

"Illegally? You have to know where to go and lay low?"

"You'd have to survive the desert and that's no easy task." Sam knew the score.

George said, "Not only that, for your own good, you would be sure not to have the drugs on you when you get caught."

"If the chances are that you get caught, how's the getting rich plan work?"

"Do it our way. We give you what we want you to take across the line. We meet on the other side and give you a vehicle and money. You're free to go."

"Are you serious?" asked Anton. "People make money that way?"

George was insistent, "People make plenty that way. If you guys have the guts, come with us, we have a Jeep that will get us to where we need to be if you want to be in on our next *job*."

"I think the two of us need to talk, excuse us." Anita wasn't too thrilled at this latest planned escapade.

They left walking along the sandy boulevard away from the bar. Anita turned to Anton, "Are you really sure you want to do this? You know they'll kill us."

"I won't let that happen. It'll be them before us. Trust me."

"I just don't trust George."

"Sam probably could talk George out of doing anything serious. It appears he's only his sidekick."

"Trouble is Anton, Sam must owe George big time and if that's the case, George will call the shots. I mean shots that will kill us. Think about it, do you really know what you are getting us into."

"I'll keep us safe. Don't worry about it. We can do this and we only have to do it once."

"I'm not sure about you Anton. Don't we need real ammunition?"

"How would they know what we have?"

Chapter Ten
Dust & Wind

Dry desert air and dusty sand blew up everywhere. Both Anton and Anita sat in the back of the dilapidated Jeep with George and Sam driving across the desert over bumpy roads, hitting pothole after pothole. Stopping at roadside stands for a few tacos and sodas. It took them days to reach their destination.

"You really have to acquire a taste for this stuff. Ground beef and cheese every day of your life?" as Anita had begun to dislike what they were eating. Besides, she wasn't sure anymore how she felt. She just wanted everything to be over sooner than later.

"That isn't all these people eat. They can cook up a storm with chicken and beef dishes that even you couldn't get enough of. After we've done with this deal, you'll be able to afford whatever it is you want." George was convinced these would be comforting words.

It seemed to please Anton as they continued along the rugged road toward the US border.

Anita dozed off as she laid her head on Anton's lap. George and Sam traded off the driving. Finally, they arrived at what Sam said would be their destination.

The town on one side had nothing but storefronts with clerks standing behind stalls. Fancy pottery, jewelry and brand name counterfeit purses, all set up for tourists, who would stroll the boardwalk. It was the time to barter, seeing how low the merchant's prices would go. The cost was minimal, the experience priceless.

"Can we stop for the night before we try anything further?" asked Anita.

"We just have time to get a drink at the bar and then we need to get into this dust storm that has followed us up the coast and is already brewing for our get-a-way. No time left for much else. Sam will give you the bag to carry across. We'll come across the main entrance crossing and meet you on the other side."

"The payoff?" asked Anton.

"We'll have it with us."

"How about the Jeep? I need the jeep when we get there."

"We're taking it across with us. You need to walk across and remain undetected. We'll give you this jeep when we meet you on the other side. We'll pay you for the bag. Then you can go. All we want is that bag."

Anton realized he and Anita had succeeded in the Jewel heist so why couldn't they succeed in doing the one *drug drop* and then just go on their way?

The four of them spent some time in the bar drinking tequila when Anita said, "I don't think that's a good idea for me Anton. I'm pregnant now."

"You're what?"

"You heard me. I guess I hid it very well with all this loose clothing. I wanted not to deliver until we get across the line."

They waited around as long as they could, when George said, "I think you two had better walk across now. Like we said, we'll meet you on the other side."

"I have a pregnant wife, George. Be aware it could take us more time to get there."

"Let's get some food and find a place to pour water on my face, Anton."

"We'll be gone a bit before we join up with you guys. My girl needs a break."

"We have to get going to catch up with the wind storm. I'll give you an hour."

For the moment the two were alone, "You realize, Anton that we still haven't found the black market for the jewels."

"I know. We have to lose George and Sam for a bit, so I can find a jeweler here that would be interested, I don't want to wait until we are in the States. It will be harder there."

"I don't think they want to wait. They say the wind won't last so the chances are we would have to wait around for another storm. That could take months."

Anton walked back to where George and Sam were waiting, "You said we could have one hour before we start. Anita and I are going to take that time."

George wouldn't let it go. "You have to be as quick as you can for all this to fit together. Pregnant or not, you need to make it across the border now."

"You said there is evidence of an old adobe building we are supposed to meet you at?"

"That's right, you will stay there until we come. Here, take this sack and be sure it is with you when we see you on the other side."

"Pardon me, George and Sam, but I have to use the *aseos*." Anita needed to make a delay for Anton to find his underground market for the jewels.

Minutes later, Anita saw Anton waiting alone. "Are they gone?"

"They are. Where's the nearest jeweler?" Anton enquired of the bar tender.

"Next door, can I help?"

"Don't think so."

"You want a ring for your lady?"

Anton asked, "You deal in jewels?"

"Are you buying me a ring?"

"Come with me and you will see."

They were now in the back of the bar when Anton asked, "Who is the jeweler I am supposed to deal with?"

"I'm the boss here. What do you have? You can afford this ring?"

Anton opened the satchel.

The bar boss couldn't believe his eyes. "I'll give you $50,000 American dollars."

"It's worth a couple million. I need a better offer."

"My best offer, $500,000. Take or leave it."

Anita stepped in, "Here's the thing, you give me your best diamond ring for our engagement and we keep one or two of the diamonds and they're yours with your offer of money."

"Are you sure you want to start that low?"

"Do it."

The exchange was made.

"Tell me, where's the nearest minister, Sir?"
"You're going to get married?"
"We are. Thank you."
"Just around the corner, you'll find the clérigo"

Anton and Anita left with the ring, elated that they had finally unloaded the jewels.

"We need to find the Chapel that's supposed to be around the corner so we can get married. Do you want to do that Anita?"

"I do. Let's do it now. We need to hurry if we want to meet up with George and Sam."

While the marriage was being performed, the bar Tender-Jeweler walked out the back of his store where George and Sam where waiting. "What's up, man? Did those two make a deal with you as well?"

"They sold jewels to me. They're off to the Chapel to get married but they plan to deliver the drugs you both agreed on. They now are carrying $500,000 cash from me and still have a couple of the diamonds."

"Got it. Keep an eye on those two to be sure they cross the border with the stash and don't double cross us. We'll take care of the rest." George now wanted more than just the stash. He had a gold mine if he played it right.

Chapter Eleven
The Delivery

"Do you realize, we will only have two of the diamonds to remind us of this part of our journey, Anton?"

"I do but sometimes I wish we gave them all to that man." Anita sighed.

"I guess that about wraps up the jewel heist but now we have to make our delivery."

"Here's an idea, Anton, why don't we just dump George and Sam, like disappear? We have money. We could just leave the drug bag with the bar tender. Disappear and find our own way across the border on our own."

"You think the bar tender will keep his mouth shut as we run for our lives? Where do we run to? No matter where we go they'll find us. They know every pebble from here to the border. No, I think we have to make that delivery, Anita. Can't let them know what we have. We have to make everything disappear."

They quickly made it back into their motel room as Anita crashed. She was pregnant and needed the rest.

Anton couldn't drop his uneasiness. He knew they had to get going with the stash he was carrying with him. He decided his anxiousness would disappear once the delivery had been accomplished. "We need to go. Those guys aren't about to wait without coming after us."

"This is going to be tough for me, Anton. That's a long way for a pregnant woman and could bring the baby here too quickly."

"We have to go."

The setting sun was hidden with the wind blowing at 60 miles an hour, sometimes as much as 80, pushing the sand into what is often called a *Haboob,* or a large heavy dust storm. Anton and Anita struggled to forge through what appeared to be a local rancher's property as they crossed over a wire fence. It didn't stop there. They heard the sounds of cattle. Anita hung on to Anton brushing past a few head of cattle though they were barely visible.

"George and Sam certainly knew what they were talking about. There isn't a border patrol cop looking for anyone about now, like they said, Security was relatively ineffective. This certainly was an opportune time for smugglers."

"Here's another wire fence, can you make it, Anita?"

Anita wasn't complaining knowing Anton had promised her this should be the last trade they would make. There would be no others but she was concerned for her baby, knowing she needed to make it to a hospital quickly. They were already on the US side.

"I'll be fine, Anton but you have to know, I need a hospital as soon as possible. I think the baby will insist on coming sooner than later."

"George said if we just came straight through, and by the looks of the map they gave us, we have to go left, where we should stumble on the adobe walls."

Struggling over cacti and scrub brush along the way, they continued on. "I just bumped into something. Could this be it, Anton?"

"Near as I can tell, it looks like part of an adobe wall. Must be it, don't you think Anita?"

"I don't think I can go any further, Anton."

"Doesn't look like much more than dilapidated adobe mud bricks. We could rest there until George and Sam show up with the jeep."

The wind continued blowing relentlessly.

"This must be it all right, Anita. Let's make a place for you to rest."

Anton and Anita pulled branches that had blown about from the nearby scrubby desert trees to make a spot for them to rest. "Do you still have the *loot,* Anton?"

"Actually, the two jewels are sown into your clothes along with the money. You're wearing the ring and I have the sack of drugs."

"Where's the money?"

"Some of it is with me under my shirt and the rest is with you."

"So we're about even."

"When they pay, they get the drugs. They are not looking for jewels and you being pregnant wouldn't alarm anyone."

"When did you put the diamonds in my clothes?"

"When we were at the hotel while you were resting."

"Why didn't you tell me?"

"Don't worry about it, we've crossed the line, we should have made it already."

"But if the baby comes too soon?"

"Don't tell me!"

"Settle down, Anton. If we can get a car and to a local hospital is all I want."

For the moment the two of them settled in the desert brush in the cool evening breeze. It wasn't hot anymore but for a pregnant woman it was uncomfortable.

"Why did we even get into this way of making a living anyhow, we already had enough money?"

"Excitement, fast money and we would get to America with a big payoff. Buy a house and live the *American Dream.* Let it go and forget the past."

"Think those guys will let us be?"

"They said this would only be a one-time deal. That was the plan."

"Do we still have all our pictures we brought with us?"

"We do. I have a small camera so if the baby comes too soon, we'll take some pictures."

A few hours passed by but Anita was beginning to feel anxious. Still, nothing was stirring, seemingly uneventful enough as they lay on the brush.

Then, "Oh Anton, my baby is coming!"

"How far apart are your labor pains?"

"No, Anton, the baby is coming now."

"I'm not surprised. Here, let me help you deliver our baby." It didn't take long for Anita to deliver her first baby.

It wasn't very sanitary but Anita was hoping they'd get to a hospital soon.

Anton had the baby in his arms. "What will we call her, Anita?"

"A girl? Call her Tabatha, I like that name."

"Here, I'm taking a picture of her in your arms. I have a pad of paper in my shirt pocket. I'll write the date and hour of her birth on it. Then when we get to the hospital, we can get it recorded."

"You will make a good father for Tabatha. Give me your camera, I want to take your picture as well."

"You think so? Let's take a *selfie*." They huddled together as Anton snapped a picture.

"We just need to get out of here, though. Anton, I'm not doing well, I need a hospital. Could be I've gotten an infection from no sterilization."

Anita's breathing wasn't good, but what could Anton do? They were in the middle of nowhere, waiting.

They not only had delivered a baby but now they were waiting to make a drug delivery. Would it be too late for Anita? How would Tabatha fair? They needed a hospital and it needed to be now.

Chapter Twelve
Fire Power

"It must be them, Anton."

"I hear that, it still sounds like they are a little way off but listen, I hear more."

"Yeah, I hear more than one person, like maybe people are being pursued. It has to be. I guess they would have to have more than one if they are giving the Jeep to us. Too bad the visibility is still so bad, can't see a thing."

"That was a bullet! I'm sure of it. Anton, get down!"

"Here, Anita, get under the brush, it's an ambush. We didn't plan on that."

Within minutes, men in combat gear appeared and began kicking the brush.

"Stop that men. My wife is under there."

One of them demanded the sack. "Give me that."

"That isn't yours. We are to meet someone else here with the cash."

He continued kicking the brush and shoving it across the desert until Anita and her baby was completely uncovered.

"What's going on? What are you doing?"

"Give us your money."

"Money?"

Anton wasn't handing anything over. "Give me the jeep, my wife delivered her baby and we need to get her to the nearest hospital. We only have enough money to pay the hospital bill."

The man in combat gear pointed the gun at him. "Sam find the money, grab their stuff."

While Anton bent down to pull the money from his back pack, shots began spraying in every direction. Suddenly Anton slumping over Anita's body as she lay on the ground holding the baby.

"What are you doing?" The baby was screaming as Anita looked up at the men. "You have all the money and the drugs. Just go." Anita held tightly on to her baby as she tried to pull herself up off the ground, Anton's body slid to the ground. Anita clutched the adobe brick wall to steady herself but she had already lost too much blood.

"Anton, please help me! Anton, Anton! Speak to me."

"Forget it woman. He's already dead. Hand over the money."

"I don't have any money, you have everything. That's all I had. Please, I need to get to the hospital now."

"Give me your money. Give it up."

"It'll be in her clothes, rip them off her."

"I'm not touching her. She's in need of a hospital. Let's get out of here."

"I want the money."

"Anton's already dead, what more do you want?"

Anita was insistent. "Get out of here."

The men looked at one another, "You know very well, you have the money. I want that." He began pulling the baby from Anita's arms. Anita pulled her back.

"What are you doing? Leave my baby alone, that's my baby!"

Anita turned to cover her wailing baby with a blanket she had brought with her from the motel. She struggled to push the men off her. "What are you doing? Don't take my baby! Don't take my clothes! Please don't take my baby!"

"Let's get out of here, border patrol can see us now!"

"Take the baby."

"I'm not your kidnapper. You want the baby, you do it."

"I have a good mind to give you a bullet."

"Lose your body guard? Smart move."

They had what they came for and within minutes the men disappeared but Anton lay there as the two border patrol agents began CPR.

"He's dead. We can do nothing more for him." Alex Benton, border patrol agent stopped but turned to give his attention to Anita.

Anita was in uncontrollable sobs, "Where's my baby? My baby is gone!"

Patrol officer Len Stumps stood over Anita. "She needs a doctor!"

"My baby, my baby! Where is my baby?"

It was evident that Anita had just given birth as she lay in a pool of blood, yet there was no baby and no drugs on her body, nothing. She lay there with clothes ripped to shreds. The patrol officers lay a blanket over her in attempt to keep her warm. They had found a dead man, presumably her husband and a missing baby on their hands.

"Lady, we need to get you to the hospital."

"I want my baby! I want my baby! Don't take me away, I want my baby!"

"We're looking for your baby."

"Oh God, please help me! Forgive me, I have sinned and I know I'm not worthy but my baby! God please save my baby."

"Tell us names. We need names! Give us your name. Who did this to you?"

"Bandits! I've never seen them before. They robbed me of everything. They took my baby!"

"We were supposed to meet some guys who would give us a jeep so my baby would be born in the United States." Anita gasped, "They took everything. My money and we had a bag, they took that too.

"Two people from Mexico said they would meet us here and give us a jeep so I could get to the hospital."

Anita knew the score if she were to admit that there was a drug exchange, she would be hauled off to jail and never find her baby. Anita realized this wasn't the time to confess. She wasn't sure it would matter feeling her chances for life was not likely.

"The names of the people who were to meet you here, do you know the names? Help us so we can find your baby."

"I don't think they were the ones we were to meet here."

"Who were you supposed to meet?"

"Can you give us a description of them?"

"The one was Geo… but these guys were bandits…" Anita was gasping for air by now.

"Hold on lady. The names! Can you give us names?"

"The other was S…S…" She gave a quick gasp, "but these guys were bandits. I wanted my baby to be born in America. Look, I have the pictures. Anton wrote my baby's name and birth on that paper, and here," she held up the pictures, "that proves I have a baby."

"A Polaroid Camera, good pictures. We know you gave birth. We can tell but we need the names of the people who did this to you. What names did they go by? Their last names, surnames?"

"Lady, what did they look like?"

"These guys looked like bandits with bandanas over their heads."

"Tell us about the guys who were supposed to help you."

"The one has black hair and a scare on his face. The other looks ordinary."

"Color hair of the other?"

"Dirty blonde." Anita began gasping for air again. "I want Tabatha, my baby. They took my baby." The struggling to breath was becoming harder by the minute, "Please find my baby."

Anita's breathing became irregular, then she passed out.

"Do CPR on her. We need to get her to the hospital."

"We're losing her."

"We need to be quick. There is no time to delay."

There was a border town hospital care center near, where Anita was taken.

"We didn't get enough of the names, Sergeant, we didn't get enough information!"

"It wouldn't be hard to interpret what she said."

"So what do we do? It's like finding a *needle in the haystack.*"

"An impossible task."

"Only one thing to keep in mind whoever did this is now traveling with a baby in tow."

"Two bandits and a baby?"

"Bandits will sell the baby and then how do we find her? They could take the baby back across the border. How do we find the baby then?"

"If they don't we now have a baby to find."

"Two men and a baby, we need to put an all-points bulletin out on them."

"Is the lady dying of gunshot wounds or childbirth?"

"We need to get the man to a morgue, we can't bury him here."

"But we have no baby."

"We have pictures and the record they wrote up. We will find the baby. Dead or alive, we will find the baby."

"We will have to get the DNA from both of them if we ever want to find the baby."

Chapter Thirteen
On The Farm
―――――

"I'm making dinner, Earl."
The Boosters had only been married two weeks when they were ranch sitting for a friend to find out if they would like farm life. Earl was a young police officer in their local area but his wife Ann hadn't decided when she would job hunt for a secretarial job or just busy herself in ranch life.
"Call me when dinner is ready. With all that's been happening at church and at the office, I'm a bit tired. Too many decisions to make."
"Anything happening at the police station?"
"Remember, I've been telling you about a case on which I was the arresting officer? That case was tried today."
"Did they put the man in prison then?"
"No, they didn't. He got off on a technicality. It seems he may have a mob connection. The hope is that this guy will lead us to the entire gang. Then we'll get the killers instead of their cronies."
"What about you? You're connected to this case just by arresting the man. Wouldn't that signal retaliation? Like they could send out a hit man?"
"The Judge gave him two years of probation, though. That's a long time to stay clean. It means he can't leave the county for two years and has to report on his activity. In my opinion, he was the wrong man to get caught. Personally, I think he was framed. To me he just doesn't seem the type but we think he works for the mob."
"You'd think he'd split from the gang."
"Don't think he can. That could mean curtains for him."

"How'd he ever get involved with that gang?"

"If we knew that, we'd be able to find our man."

"I'm afraid Earl. I just have that gut feeling that all isn't well."

"We'll be okay. This guy won't show his face around here. If he does, they'd throw the book at him and he's not the killer."

"But the gang he's caught up with, is."

"Yeah, but no, I don't think that will happen. For instance, we know George, he's pretty *street-savvy*. He always seems to have the inside scoop about gangs. He'll let us know if anything is coming our way."

"This all sounds too dangerous for me. I don't like it."

"I shouldn't think we would have to worry."

"Wasn't George fired from the Police force? How do you figure he'll be your *stoolie* now?"

"They might have been a bit tough on him. When it's perceived that a person might have a connection to a robbery, he has to be fired. I think he's okay but he does have *street smarts*. Should Bill's people try anything on a cop, they'll be hunted down relentlessly until the entire gang has been caught."

"I still don't like it."

Earl wasn't about to get too concerned, he wanted to get on with his evening.

"I'm going to tend to the dog."

"Dinner will be ready shortly."

"Call me when you are ready."

Earl headed for the barn looking for his dog. "Rover where are you?" He hesitated. *Well, maybe he went into the garage. I'll check that.* He continued calling. There was no answer. He opened the door but it was dark with little light seeping in through the tiny window. He reached his hand up the wall to where he figured a light switch might be.

Rover was lying in a pool of blood. "My God, someone killed my dog." Earl's heart sank. He turned when he felt the sense of a human standing next to him. Looking up he saw a man's shadow standing next to the workbench. Earl's eyes began to focus when he saw the figure of a man. Was he here to give him information?

"What are you doing here?" asked Earl.

With no explanation, the man belted Earl with a heavy blow to his stomach. Earl doubled down, "I don't get it. What have I done to you?"

"You know exactly what you did!"

Earl took another blow to the head. By now he was reeling. His plan wasn't to fight anyone off but he knew, he would have to do whatever was necessary. Punches went back and forth, in both directions.

"Come on, Earl. Give me what you have!"

"Sorry, I still don't know what this is all about. I'd rather talk this out. You know we always try to be fair and find out what the problem is. So what's up? I don't get it."

"You put Bill Thomas on probation. You wanted him tried for murder. It wasn't easy trying to get him off."

"You don't think he committed the murder?"

"Never mind that now."

"That means you are a part of the gang we are looking for? I didn't know that."

"Well, you do now."

"Back off man."

"Too late buddy!"

"You killed my dog?"

"Had to, he would've barked."

"You think you can get away with this?" Earl grabbed for his gun.

The man wasn't about to back off, using the butt of his rifle, slugging Earl across the forehead, then pulled the trigger.

Earl went down. The man disappeared.

Ann, unaware, was about to call Earl for dinner when she heard gunshots. "What was that?" She stumbled down the stairs yelling at the top of her lungs, "Earl, Earl! Earl where are you? I heard gun shots. What's going on?" She hurried over to the Garage where she spotted Rover lying dead in a pool of blood. She turned where she saw Earl's lifeless body lying on the floor.

Ann hovered over Earl's body trying in desperation to revive him, looking for any hope of life. There was nothing, no pulse, no breathing, nothing. The garage door opened.

Then she saw a man she recognized, "What are you doing here, George?"

"I heard gunfire. I thought you might need help so I came running."

"Somebody killed my dog and my husband. Why?"

"Don't know Ann but remember your husband is a cop. I heard about the trial he was a witness for."

"I told him it was going to get too dangerous." Ann was sobbing. "I need to call the cops. I have to find his killer."

"I wouldn't do that if I were you. When you call the cops, do you think they will believe you? With no one to accuse, they'll think you did it. Surely, you don't think the police will believe you when you tell them you found your husband and the dog dead? You will be interrogated until you can't take it anymore. Trust me I know what I'm talking about. You have to have an alibi and I can do that for you."

"Thank you, but I have to report it right now."

"Before you do that, we need to get our stories straight. I saw a man running from your property, disappearing in the bushes behind your house."

"You will tell the cops, that?"

"Of course, like I said, I'll be your alibi."

"Then you saw the killer?" George didn't answer. "George, did you see him? Do you remember what that person looked like?"

"No, I just saw a shadow."

The police arrived in minutes of being called. The investigation began. Questioning ensued and as George had predicted, to Ann it was grueling.

Joe Contraus and Stan Bucher arrived on scene within minutes of Ann's 911 call. "Are you sure that's how it all went down for Earl?" asked Contraus.

"Sir, you heard the lady. I know these good people and often come by to visit them. Earl was a very good friend of mine. Even I heard gunshots from the distance. It certainly wasn't Ann who did it if that's what you're thinking."

"No one is ever accused of a crime until proven guilty without a fair trial."

"Fair, I'll bet. You know you profile all the time."

"Your name, Sir, what is your name?"

"George, you remember only too well who I am."

"Remembered what, George?"

"I was a police officer before I was unfairly accused."

"We are dealing with the death of Earl Booster. We don't need your interference in our investigation. If you interfere and keep insisting, we'll need to take you into custody."

"Just don't accuse Ann."

The cops called in backup for an intensive investigation taking samples of everything.

"Is this Earl's gun, Ann?"

"That one is."

"The rifle?"

"I've never seen it before, but I wouldn't know what firearms he might have had. I didn't interfere."

"We'll have to take all of this as evidence, Stan."

They gathered everything possible, checked around the building. Hours later transport was called and Earl's body was removed. "We need to check to see what kind of firearm was used and if any of these were the ones. You will be able to pick up Earl's gun at the police station when we've checked everything out."

Ann asked, "How long do you think it will take?"

"We'll let you know but if you want, give us a call in a few days."

Everyone left and all was quiet but to Ann, nothing seemed quite right. She gave way to tears. Earl had been taken away and she would be left to bury her dog and soon her husband. What could she do next? How could she support herself with no job?

"How do you suppose I will make a living now? Earl was the bread winner."

"It's going to be all right. I have a friend who would love to hire a good looking gal like you."

Chapter Fourteen
Hiding Baby
―――――

"Just exactly what are you going to do with that baby, George?"

"We have a child that nobody wants."

"I wouldn't say nobody wants that baby. Take her to the hospital and give her a chance to life. You don't have to identify yourself, just leave the baby and disappear."

"Ah, but think about it, no one knows she even exists and the benefits we can have with her."

"When we get caught what are you going to tell the authorities? Where did you find her?"

"My answer is obvious, we rescued the baby from bandits in the desert but slow it down, Sam. We'll give her to Ann. She'll make a good mother."

"Ann? Are you sure of that?"

"Yeah, I'm her alibi, she believes I rescued her."

"How do you know she will want to rear a child that isn't hers?"

"She owes me."

"If she knows too much?"

"This is how I can keep tabs on her, I'll know her every move. She wouldn't think to refuse and it will keep her busy for a few years. She won't have time to think about what happened. When we've had enough, or Ann gets wise to us, we can always accuse her of keeping a baby that wasn't hers. That takes care of Ann. If all goes as planned, we can make good use of the child in a few years or sell her on the black market."

"You rogue, George! That's a human being and you want to sell her. You're a kidnapper, that's what you are."

"No, I'm not, I rescued her. She could have been killed."

"By your gun fire, she could have been killed."

"That's not how I see it. Those were bandits that had the fight out with Border patrol."

"In disguise."

"We rescued that baby and you want to keep that story straight! It was they who killed Anton while we were busy taking the stash owed us and when we realized they were dying we rescued the baby."

"Uh-uh."

"And how do you know they'll ever catch us? They would be looking for two guys and a baby. Passing the baby off to Ann will keep us off the hook."

"What's her name anyhow?"

"Anita called her Tabatha. Like I said, we have to keep our story straight so she's a baby we rescued from smugglers in the desert. We found her after the shoot-out. Do you remember what Anton's surname was?"

"Yeah, Rosander, but you realize, she is only a few hours old and could just as easily die if we don't get her checked out at a hospital."

"You have to be crazy, we can't do that, Sam. Take her and keep her quiet, I'm thinking."

It didn't take long for Sam to quieten the baby. It was as if he'd had experience from the past.

"If she doesn't make it, her blood will be on your hands, George. You will be responsible for her death, but then what would you care?"

"You are expendable, Sam, don't forget it."

"See how far you will get without me."

"I could always find a replacement for you, Sam."

"No one would be that great a sucker."

"Never forget I was the guy that gave you that alibi."

"I don't know why I took your bait. The more I think about it, I would never have been blamed."

"Remember, I'm paying you the bucks. Look at you. The clothes you wear compared to what you had. The places you go with me you would never have even seen before."

"Give me a break, George. I have a degree. Just got involved in too many meaningless relationships and went on a binge when you found me. You're right, the money and the places we go sounded good, but I'm regretting it."

No one said anything more as they drove into Los Angeles to find the lady called Ann Booster. Ann was now known as a good-hearted bar maid eking out a living. It was true that Ann felt she owed George big time and he had made certain that she would continue to believe it. George had persuaded her to work in a local bar. Good money, as he put it so aptly.

Just as George had predicted Ann would give the baby entrusted to her all she could possibly need while he promised to always take care of the extra needs Tabatha might have. Blackmail kept Ann exactly where he wanted her and it gave him the padding he wanted. When the time came for him to need another alibi in the future, he would demand it of her.

Every day Ann would carry Tabatha with her to the bar while she worked. People would come in and be warmed by the sight of a little baby resting in a bassinet asleep. Men toned down the words that came out of their mouths because a female baby was in their presence. A few years went by when finally, little Tabatha was put into nursery school.

"Where's our baby," a patron would ask.

"She's in nursery school. I want her to grow up smarter than you."

"You are making a good choice, Ann. Maybe she can make some smart decisions for her life and not be like the rest of us."

"Let's hope so. She will get that chance." Ann was serious.

It seemed to Ann that working at the Ranchero Bar was a good thing because George and Sam not only provided the extras for Tabatha's needs but made it a practice never to come to her place of employment. Her home was a different situation. Sam was the usual person to make contact and if George showed up it usually spelled trouble. Anytime George wanted his presence to be known, he'd stop by for coffee. Unfortunately, his presence always became combatant toward Sam. Another argument, another issue development for no reason at all but to make it a memorable scene. No denying he had been at Ann's resident. When questioned by the police, Ann would have to say, 'yes, I remember.'

Life continued on for a few more years. Every day after school Tabatha waited at the bar until Ann was done with work. She kept busy doing her homework in the boss's office and when the homework was complete, she kept herself busy reading books borrowed from the school library.

The day came when Tabatha was turning ten years old. Ann bought Tabatha a few gifts planning to celebrate at home after Ann's shift at the bar ended for the day. "We need to hurry home, Tabatha. I'm going to make you a birthday cake and I have a few gifts for you."

Tabatha was a typical ten-year old and had a hard time containing her curiosity.

"What did you get me, Mom? Please tell me, I have to know."

"Can't tell you." Her inquisition continued almost all the way home, when Ann noticed more than just Sam's car in her driveway.

"Are we going to have a party, Mom?"

"I didn't invite anyone but it looks like Sam is there." Ann knew that something wasn't right when she realized George was with Sam.

Chapter Fifteen
Time Moves On
―――――――

     That was 1994. Anita had been through a Jewelry heist, saw her husband die from gun-shot wounds and had her baby abducted. Anita was about to walk out of the hospital totally depressed not knowing where she would go and if there was a place she could go. She was being consumed with finding her baby. Peace would never be hers until she would find out what happened to Tabatha. She had already paid for the choices Anton and she had made. They had paid dearly. Yet, she was alive. Would God ever be there for her again? Had she paid enough and then what would be enough?
     That was only half of the problem. She did have a passport, but that just meant she could legally visit. Eventually she would have to leave the US but with no money to travel, how would she ever get back to Sweden and how could she leave without knowing what happened to Tabatha?
     "Anita, I have some information for you before you leave the Shelter." Dr. Tim Turner had founded the Shelter and Hospital expressly for those who ran into trouble trying to enter the US illegally but ended up with life threatening injuries. "First, I have your release papers where it's documented why you came to us." He laid out the papers for her to see what he had. "When the hospital was told by border patrol your circumstances, all your care was paid for by a local charity. You can continue to stay at the Shelter listed on this paper, which is just next door to us. Show them your release papers so that you don't have to explain. Their practice is to keep everything confidential. If anyone comes looking

for you for any reason, they will inform you and advise what you should or should not do. You'll be safe with them. They usually are willing to help you get yourself together and maybe they will be able to answer your questions. In some cases, they help with the immigration." Turner released her to his nurse and left.

Anita sat there after she gave all the thanks to her Doctor she could. Nurse Lydia sat there with her for a moment. "If I have to go back to Sweden, how do I even do that if I can't work here? How do I qualify for a *green card?*"

Lydia attempting to sound hopeful, "I have an idea that you aren't the first that has come to this mission hospital with non-U.S. Status that needed assistance. I'm sure if you talk to the Doc, he will know where and how to give you direction. Remember, God doesn't give up on us and He's not about to give up on you no matter how bad it got for you or what choices you made. I'll bet someday you'll even find your baby."

Anita's face lit up. "You mean there is hope for me?"

"You are on the right side of the grass, aren't you? You should have died but you didn't. You are still the beautiful gal you were before all this happened. There is hope for you. I want you to remember that when you find your baby, tell me. Please promise you will do that?"

"I will do that, you have my word, no matter how far I have to go, or how long it takes, Lydia. I will find you."

A word of hope was what Anita needed. Those were only a few words, but maybe she could find God. She just had too. Anita's scars were no longer visible anymore but they still hurt on the inside.

Arriving at the shelter early in the afternoon, Anita sat in the lobby trying to think of what she would say in her own defense for surely they would want to know her life story. It still hurt, how could she talk?

"Let's get you checked in. My name is Mary Kent and I'll do that for you."

It wasn't long before things began to settle as she worked for her keep at the Shelter. She was learning and caring for others while she waited. Then one day, she became the lamb that God had been looking for, she found her Savior. Soon a year had gone by but she had grown inwardly and started feeling stronger.

Then came that restless feeling again. This time she wanted to find her baby. Tabatha had to be somewhere, but where? Yes, her daughter had been abducted. That realization was unrelenting.

"I know you are restless and I don't figure I'd be any different."

"You noticed, Doctor Tim?"

The Doctor sat across from Anita at dinner in the Shelter. "I haven't heard anymore from the border patrol."

"That might be just part of the problem. If I go back to Sweden, what happens to my finding Tabatha? I need to go to immigration and see if they will give me any leniency. Do you think they will understand?"

"If I go and be your sponsor?"

"Are you really sure you want to do that for me?"

"You know, Anita, you are *growing on me* and then I think I'm not sure I want you to go away."

"What are you saying?"

"We've never even had a date but I'm afraid if I ask, you may think I have an ulterior motive. If, however, I became your sponsor, you and I could start looking for Tabatha."

"An offer I couldn't resist. I have to find Tabatha. How can I say no?"

"You've been here already a few years."

"A few years? I thought it was only one year?"

"No, it's been a long time."

"there is just one problem. I'm going to be charged for possession of drugs as well as smuggling them across into the US. When that happens I'll never be allowed back in and there goes my finding Tabatha."

"I work with the hospital you were in, as well. They have never charged you with anything. The authorities know you are here but I'm thinking there just might be more to the story than we know."

"Why is that?"

"They could be looking for the perpetrators. Remember, someone tried to kill you and they managed to kill your husband. Sending you back doesn't help them find the murderer. You also, still have your passport."

"And because I don't have a real job, I'm still visiting?"

"I have means, Anita."

"You can't leave here."

"Oh, yes I can. The people here know what they are doing. They are all very well trained and I can keep tabs on them while we go looking."

"I'm supposed to trust you?"

"No fear, I'm not about to do anything, I care for you too much. My greatest joy would be finding Tabatha. It's not like I'm leaving the Shelter *high and dry*, I'd just be gone for a bit."

"I just don't know. Tabatha won't know me anymore and it could take years for me to find her. Then think about it, I still have to tell her my story."

"Let's look at the facts, Anita. You say you and Anton smuggled drugs into this country. When you were rescued you had lost your baby and your husband was shot dead. You were given up for dead. When you were found you had your clothes ripped off. You had nothing, no evidence as to what you are telling me. No evidence to charge you on."

"How can you possibly leave? You are the doctor on call. How can the Shelter do without you?"

"Charles helps out a lot too and he's a qualified doctor, so that's not a problem, either."

"It might take years and I'm still not a legal citizen."

"I can help you get your papers together will we search for Tabatha."

"What about your family? Your wife, how could she let you go?"

"Anita, I'm not married. I've devoted my entire life to helping people and somehow having a family was never in the plan. I always thought I'd eventually go into a third world country. Then I starting the shelter here, close to the border, a small town which seemed the way to go."

"Then I can't understand your leaving this place."

"I've heard so much about your heart being torn apart by your daughter being abducted that I would love to be a part of that plan. If God would permit me to do that, it would be my calling, at least until we could find her."

"I don't even know where to start. Where do I start? Like I said, it could take years."

"It could take years, but helping people does take time. It takes a lifetime when God calls you to that mission. I want to answer his call. Will you let me?"

Chapter Sixteen
The Search Begins

───────

"What do we do with this Doctor and wife that are looking for their daughter? They insist on answers and intend to do their own investigations but want us to give them any information we have."

"Don't know. It's going to take a *rocket scientist* to figure this one out."

In Stump's office there was countless files from floor to ceiling filled with boxes containing files with information about every homicide or accident that had happened over the years. The two officers began pulling files of everything for the year and day of Anita's arrival in their town.

"Abduction, what do we have that might give us a head start on what they want to know."

There it was, a file for Anita Bergin. "Got it. Did you look at it Stumps?"

"Yeah, and there is a file on her husband, Anton Rosander. We were the ones on scene that day, Benton. Do you remember that?"

"I thought that lady died."

"Remember we took her to that clinic? We thought for sure she couldn't possibly make it."

"Look at this recording, a note saying a couple of suspicious men came around inquiring if Anita had died. The shelter didn't release any information but wanted them to come to us. It seems their names were George and Sam."

"I remember that but when we checked that out, they already had disappeared."

"Look, this must be the lady's ring. That's a beauty, her husband must have really cared. Here's pictures and notes about their daughter."

"I want to keep that for their daughter."

"We are going to find her?"

"You bet, we'll find her."

Alex Benton and Len Stumps were convinced that if Anita had been able to pull through the ambush, they would never give up on the hunt for her daughter.

"Stumps, look at these files. We have some time before the Doctor and Anita arrive. These all seem to have happened in that time frame, like the same year."

"Bill Thomas' profile for instance, Stumps, did you see this?"

"Yeah, but I don't get the connection. Isn't he supposed to be a CPA and was doing the books for a firm called George's Stationery Firm."

"There's that name again."

"Wasn't it Officer Earl Booster who was called to that office when he found a dead body in one of the adjoining rooms?"

"Who tipped them off about that one?"

"Apparently, an anonymous phone call. The Officers on duty obtained a search warrant."

"The strange part is, Thomas claims he knew nothing yet they found his pen with his wallet lying next to the body. The pen had his name inscribed as a CPA. He's apparently the man who does the financial books for the firm. The officers on scene questioned him about his being there. Thomas says he came to work in the morning, hadn't checked any of the offices, didn't even know his wallet was missing. The owner was question and of course, he had an alibi. No one seems to know who put the body in that room. The only figure prints found on the wallet were from Thomas. Evidently he was booked."

"They obviously would have accused him."

"They did but it was only circumstantial evidence."

"That wouldn't hold up in court."

"Booster wanted him to talk. Tell what he knew, who he was working for. He wouldn't cooperate in that regard. With no one else, and knowing he was aware of the perpetrator, the judge gave him two years' probation. He wasn't out on probation a couple of hours and Booster turns up dead and everyone has an alibi."

"Something is surely wrong with that picture."

"Yeah, but somehow we need proof."

"We do but now it has already been ten years."

Neither Stumps nor Benton knew what to think of the recent unanswered homicide. It wasn't a rare occurrence but this one seemed to have connections.

"The fact that some of this stuff has the ear-marks of connections means we need to start tracking everyone that was in that time frame. Those who happened to be near any of this in spite of the reported alibis. With that killing ten years ago and now we've had a few more unanswered homicides, I think we need to bear down on them."

"I agree and get the gut feeling there are connections. With whom, I don't know."

"Anita may be able to tell us who those guys were. At least, if she didn't lose her memory, she might be able to give us names."

"Why did she wait ten years to start looking for her daughter?"

"It took a long time for Anita to get well enough to even hope of a normal life. Then after all that it took a while for her to get her legal documents."

"She could have just married a US Citizen."

"Give me a break Stumps. You still have to have a *green card* first to become a citizen."

"Let's inform them of the information we have now."

"Here, one more file. This one could be interesting. Look at the log Cortraus left with us."

"It's also been ten years since Joe Cortraus retired. He left shortly after the border fiasco went down, but look what he wrote in his log. Apparently he went to the Ranchero Bar for his usual drink after work. It says he noticed a new bar maid who served him. She says her name is Ann. He realizes that Ann is Earl's widow. He says he didn't say anything but he thinks someone should check this out. But then, why would they since no one is doing anything wrong. At least Ann isn't."

"Look, a couple weeks later he wrote that she brought a baby to work. He says she hadn't even looked or acted as though she was pregnant. He goes on to say that Earl and Ann weren't married more than a couple of weeks when Earl was killed and then suddenly she shows up with a new born baby she calls Tabatha."

"Tabatha!"

Stumps and Benton looked at one another.

Chapter Seventeen
Trek to Chicago

"Just what are you doing here, George? What do I have to do for you now?"

"We're moving you to another home, Ann. Pack up and let's get out of here."

"Why?"

Tabatha spoke up, "I'm not moving!"

"Shut up kid. You'll get locked up if you sass me!"

"You'll do no such thing as long as I'm around."

"You're only around as long as I say so."

Ann took Tabatha by the hand. "Here take this." Ann gave her the small grocery bag. "Go take this sack into the house and start your homework while I sort out what we are doing. Mommy will see that we are fine." Tabatha ran into the house.

Sam answered, "It's getting a little hot here for us. George decided Tabatha needs a father in another city."

"Sorry Guys, I'm not getting married to anyone you choose for me."

"We aren't asking you to marry him, we just want a home for both you and Tabatha. Show everyone you are a family. We don't care if you love or hate one another we just want a nice home for you and the kid."

"I don't get it. Who is the guy?"

"You'll find out. He's already waiting for you and Tabatha to come. We have a long trek ahead of us. Pack up and come with us. It will take a few days to get to Chicago."

"It's Tabatha's birthday. We were going to celebrate and not only that, I can't just take her out of school without notifying anyone."

"We already did that for you today. After Tabatha left school we went in and notified them of everything."

"How could you do that, I'm supposed to be the parent."

Sam spoke up, "What you should know is that George has a notarized copy that he is one of the guardians for Tabatha."

"And if Tabatha and I don't go with you?"

"You have no choice. You don't come, no Tabatha. Like I said, George will lock her up until he finds your replacement. The outcome for you wouldn't be so good either. You better do what the boss wants, Ann."

"Who would be my replacement? Who did you have in mind?" Ann was considering her options.

"It wouldn't be your concern, now would it?" George was angry by and he didn't appreciate being questioned.

Reluctantly, Ann complied. She couldn't accept the fact that George and Sam would find yet another home for a helpless child and she knew full well, it wouldn't faze them to lock Tabatha up. They had threatened that many times but Ann played interference.

Tabatha was standing in the doorway listening. Sam turned to Tabatha commenting, "It's what George wants."

"So then George, what kind of man would this be?"

"That shouldn't worry you. We just merely want the appearance of a family. What you do will be your own business."

"You're going to have to pay for schooling and I want an excellent education for her Tabatha."

"You can talk to Sam about that. Whatever he thinks, we'll make happen. Myself, I'm not interested. I'm too busy making money."

"If you don't like it, treat it as a make believe father for Tabatha." Sam didn't seem concerned.

Sam and George were gone but Ann knew that they would return expecting Ann and Tabatha to be packed and ready in less than an hour. She tried to explain the details to Tabatha.

"Make believe? What's a make believe father?"

"I don't think I know that answer, Tabatha. We're going to where the snow comes in the winter, which they said will be Chicago."

"I'm not going, Mother."

"And just where do you think you would be going if not with me?"

"I don't know but I'm not going."

"Tabatha, sit down and let me tell you the score. You and I don't get to go free for a long time. Maybe someday when you are ready for college, we can work on a plan. If I follow your wishes now, we're dead."

Tabatha looked at her mother in shock. What did she mean? She knew her mother didn't ever mince words. She knew what she was talking about but Tabatha didn't. "Dead, as in life is over?"

"You've got it!"

"What have I done to them? Why would they do that to you and me?"

"For now, all I can tell you, they are not good people."

"Then run away with me."

"Can't do that, they'll hunt us down one way or another. I'm not worried about me but I promised God I would take care of you."

"Mother, I just know we shouldn't go with them."

"Sorry, we have no choice."

Tabatha heard more than her mother was volunteering in information. *These people have to be killers. Mother said as much. God, I need you now more than ever. Make me your child and show me a way of escaping but include Mother in the plan.*

It was a tiring journey especially for Ann and Tabatha. George and Sam would stop at the most unforgiving motels along the way. They didn't care about them much less about themselves. They just had to be gangster, Tabatha was sure of it. Their preference was to spend only enough on Tabatha and Ann to keep them from starving otherwise desperation could cause them to run. How could anyone enjoy such a trek?

Tabatha had learned from her mother to hold her tongue and keep her inquisitive mind to herself. Her mother would answer anything she would like to know when they were alone but not while George and Sam were present. If this was what constituted a *make believe family,* Ann very emphatically advised her never to trust any of the men that came near them. Church would be her only out other than school. When her mother was not available she would need to find her way to the bar where Ann was employed. So far the plan had worked.

"Don't worry, Ann. Soon we will be there and we have a house secured. It has three bedrooms and two bathrooms. Tabatha can have her own space. For you Ann, Bill Thomas is a good man. He will come and go as he pleases. There is also a job in the local Tavern for you. It will be good for all of us."

Ann answered, "I'm excited."

George was about to lose his cool. "I have a mind to just drop all of you off here in the middle of nowhere and see if you like that."

"What a relief that would be. I promise you'd never get any problems from me. I know nothing."

"Stop it Ann and George. It is enough. No one cares anymore except for you George. You had to get out of town and now you have to work with a family to disguise yourself. Just stop the fight and be glad we are all here to pull that off."

"Then why, George, didn't you find your own woman? Then you would've had your own family and you could let us be."

"Stop it, both of you. Don't trust George, so just stop it." Sam was adamant.

Ann was quiet. *So that was it, another blackmail job. He is never going to give me my freedom back.*

"Here it is, Chicago." Sam was relieved the drive was over.

They settled into a little house that had been abandoned for a good many years. Ann and Tabatha would clean it up and persuaded Sam to supply the paint and tools. Ann and Bill settled into separate rooms while Tabatha had the upstairs room with a connecting bathroom. The house had been an old dilapidated rundown deluxe home that hadn't been occupied in many years.

"At least it's clean. Let's do the walk-in closet now."

Bill demanded, "No, do not touch that, it doesn't go anywhere. It's to stay out of bounds."

So it was for the next few years. No questions, no answers.

Time continued on for a few more years but the *oven* began to heat up yet again and Tabatha was about to turn 16 in May.

Chapter Eighteen
Slipped By

"It's becoming impossible to track the people that ambushed you that day in the desert. When we first talked to you that day, you weren't much help."

"Wow, it's been too many years. How long do you think it'll be until we find my daughter?"

"That might very well depend on how much help you can give us."

"I'll tell you everything I know." She turned to Tim, "Is that what I should do?"

"Try answering the Officer's questions but I don't think they want your life's story for now."

Stumps and Benton looked at one another. Shouldn't they want to know everything? Stumps started the questions, "Do you still remember anything at all of the day of the ambush?"

"You have to understand I was totally wrapped around my baby being snatched out of my arms."

Tim added, "When she came to us at the clinic, she was unconscious. It took weeks for her to regain consciousness and then all I heard for a month was, 'where's my baby.'"

Officer Benton started, "Let's see if we can maybe get you to remember. The names of those people you had contact with, do you remember them?"

"Okay, I remember before the ambush. Anton and I drove up from Mexico City in George and Sam's Jeep."

"What brought you into the US side?"

"I was pregnant and the guys said they would give us the Jeep to get me to the hospital where I wanted my baby to be born. Instead, we encountered an ambush. I don't remember if George and Sam ever showed. All I can see in my mind is men in fatigues grabbing at everything we had and then they grabbed my baby."

"How is it that you drove up from Mexico City with them. Did you know them well, did you and your husband work for them at some time?"

"No, I'm sure Anton didn't know them before Mexico City. We would have met in Mexico City and I know they drove us up to the border."

"The only way we will ever find them is that they still are together." Stumps was hoping for the best scenario.

"You think it was them? You mean they took my baby?"

"That's what we think. Our best guess would be that they would still have Tabatha or know where she is."

Stumps decided they would break for the day and reconvene the next day. "My forensic expert will be here tomorrow. Let's start early tomorrow."

They went home but Anita had a heavy heart. How could she relax? She wanted to run and just go. Run and find Tabatha.

"Tim, they could have sold her for money if she even is alive."

"Likely they want her to get a little older. She'll be more profitable to them."

"Don't say that, it hurts."

"I know, but it's our only chance, Anita. It's our only chance."

Tim wasn't blind but his heart began to stir. Was he spending too much time with Anita? He didn't even know if she had feelings for him. His primary mission had not changed but his heart had. Maybe he needed to back off and let someone else continue the search. Dare he talk to her about his plight? Maybe it was being in separate rooms? Still the rooms were adjoining and they had agreed they wouldn't do anything without the other knowing ahead of time.

The morning was refreshing at the break of dawn. The sun was up and they would be on to the police department to see if they could have a conversation about the two men called George and Sam. It was a long shot but it would be something they had to do.

There again, they sat and waited. Finally, the forensic specialist came in with a couple of large bound books full of pictures.

"We have some information here. We have pictures, Anita. Do you think you can make identification from them?"

"Wow, it's been awhile. I don't know."

"Want to try?"

"See if you can." Tim insisted.

There were many. Anita looked. Sometimes she seemed confused. She would look again. They began looking through volumes of books with pictures. After hours of looking through mug shots, there it was. The scar, it had to be that scar. "That's it, Tim, look at these pictures."

Officer Jim pulled the records on the chosen person Anita seemed to recognize.

"Here's the scoop, if you recognized him, what about these two?"

"Is that Sam?"

"It is. What about this one?"

"I have never seen him before."

The Doctor couldn't be contained, "They could be the two people that came to the Hospital after Anita admitted. I'm sure of it."

"Okay," Officer Jim continued. "George is dangerous. He was a police officer but was caught *pushing* drugs. That wasn't bad enough but we have reason to believe he was involved in several fatalities. However, we have traced his presence at several homicides but each time he has a solid alibi and as a result, he could never be charged. Someone always stands up for him. We think there is a trio, George, Sam and Bill. Bill seems to be the business head, George does the killing and Sam is the go-between to keep George looking good."

Tim asked, "Where are they now?"

"We tracked them down to where we could do a stake out but somehow they seem to pick up on it and then disappear again."

"You think it's an inside job?"

"No, we don't seem to think that but he does still have connections with other police officers. We don't know if somehow he is able to get the information from them."

Anita sat there listening. "The killings, are they drug related?"

"It appears to be every time. We've been on their trail now for almost ten years. Just when it seems like it will become a *cold case* we hear of them again. Another killing and there they are with another alibi."

"I don't get it." Anita insisted, "Who gives them the alibi?"

Tim answered, "Blackmail."

Officer Jim responded, "Exactly. Only one thing, just maybe Anita, you could identify and be the witness to them this time."

"If I do that, I'll be recognized and end up being the accused by them. They would want to know my connection and before you know it, I'm the one who is prosecuted."

"We don't have to let that happen."

It was as though Dr. Tim Turner could have been an attorney. "We stay clear of anything until we get Tabatha. We get Tabatha and Anita gets total clemency. Then and only then, Anita can be the witness."

"We can work on that."

"No, we have to have that answer before we proceed and we need all this in writing. In the first place, you have no evidence to hold against Anita but we want everything in writing so that we can continue."

Officer Jim sat back in his chair. "Why would you need anything if we have no evidence?"

"How do you think George gets his alibis? My thinking is that he will find a way to turn the tables. I refuse to let that happen to Anita."

"I get the picture."

"The next question we have, where is Tabatha?"

"We don't know."

"Tell me, why are we doing this? All we want is Tabatha."

"Could be if you witness against George, it might just be disclosed. I have a hunch, if George gets a conviction for murder, Sam and Bill will be willing to tell us all that happened in a plea deal."

"It is a gamble, Anita. Do you want to take it? We might want to talk later."

"Oh, Tim, I'd do anything to find Tabatha. Where do we go from here, officer Jim? Where do we go from here?"

"It was getting too hot for him here. Now that we figure it is likely to be these three guys, we have a lead to go on. We'll do some digging and let you know what we come up with."

Anita was in a quandary. She had a sensitive heart but what now? With no real answers as to the whereabouts these men may have taken Tabatha, how would she ever be found? Did this mean that Dr. Tim Turner would drop out of her life? If he did, she would have to go it alone but how could she? She had no idea what she needed to do next. Then again, God had rescued her before and she knew God was faithful so He would do it again.

Tim and Anita were outside the police station facing one another. "What was it you wanted to discuss with me?" Anita's mind was spinning. "I know what you are thinking, I may never find Tabatha. You have to be tired of helping me. I totally understand that you need to get back to the Shelter and you probably think I could work this out by myself. I probably should, shouldn't I?"

"Are you done talking?"

"No, because I don't know where to start."

"I want to propose to you."

"You what?"

"I love you. I want you to be my wife. Please, I don't ever want to lose you. Do you think you could learn to love me? Do I even have a chance?"

"Oh, Tim do you mean that?"

"I do, please tell me you will."

Chapter Nineteen
Traversing the Plaines

"One more motel! When do we reach the end of the line?"

"Anita, Anita, my dear sweet Anita, we are going to find Tabatha. She's here somewhere."

"Behind the bushes, I know." Anita was exhausted from the driving with no end in sight. "If those guys ever get wind of our chasing them down, we risk being killed."

"Even if they were face to face with you, they would believe you were only a figment of their imagination. Huh, come to think of it, maybe they would repent?"

"Only in your dreams! That means you think it was the two of them that ambushed us?"

"I do but If we think we are close to finding them, then we have to notify the authorities, that's the plan. We call the detectives in the Police Department. They investigate and we wait."

"Give them another chance to disappear. They won't stand around for cops to show up. I don't have to be a genius to figure that out."

"We don't plan for that to happen. It's all about surprises."

"Surprise attack? I wouldn't even know what Tabatha looks like anymore. I can barely remember what Anton looked like. We were together only a couple of years. Married for only a day."

"If we can flush out the man with the scar, everything will begin to fit together like a puzzle."

"Are we checking out this bar?"

"Let's."

Anita wasn't sure about Tim. After all he was the Doctor. He was dignified and could easily be spotted as *not being one of them.*

"Before we do this Tim, let's do a *make-over* on you. I could do with that too."

"*Make-over?*"

"Yeah, you're too dressed up. Any mobster is going to know you are looking for something and possibly for someone."

"What do you suggest?"

"I spotted a western store just a few doors down. Come."

It wasn't long before both looked like Cowboy and Cowgirl. "Still a problem."

"What?"

"Need some dirt on your shoes and maybe your sleeves. Let's do that."

They did a little messing up and soon were prepared to enter the hard-core investigating or at least to gather information. "I know the *bar* scene from my past life so follow my lead."

"I remember that story."

They sauntered in as though this was familiar ground for them. "You the boss around here?" inquired Anita.

"What, you want a job?"

"Naw, you wouldn't be busy enough to hire another bar maid."

"We get plenty busy in the night."

"What ya' paying?"

"If ya' serious, I'll get the boss."

"I'm just joking with you. Tim and I are sort of passing through. But I need some info." Anita grabbed a napkin off the counter. "I want to sketch a picture of a person I hope you can tell be something about."

Tim wasn't sure of himself anymore. He didn't know she could come up with a description, let alone draw a picture of a man she now hadn't seen for many years.

Anita began the drawing. "He had black hair and a scar on his left cheek. This is how I remember he looked."

"What was the color of his hair?"

"Black."

"Does he travel with a side kick?"

"He does and isn't his name Sam?"

"Yeah, I've seen them. But I'm not sure. The only connection I ever had, was when three guys came by and asked if I'd hire a young lady by the name of Ann."

"Ann?"

"She worked for me for a few years. Shortly after she started working here, suddenly she started showing up with a baby. I didn't even know she was pregnant. I didn't have a problem with that because somehow the bar started getting saner whenever the baby slept in her basket on the counter. My clientele seemed to like that. Business continued to be good and somehow Ann proved to be good with both the customers and the baby."

"What was the baby's name? Could you remember that?"

"I didn't really pay any attention to that but maybe our bartender remembers. Let me ask him."

"Dan, can you come here?"

"How can I help?"

"Remember Ann?"

"I do. What was her baby's name?"

"Tabatha."

"You know that for sure?"

"Don't, but that's what everybody called her. Maybe it was just what our customers called her but Ann never objected to that name."

Dan continued, "Then just like that, they were gone. Didn't even say good-bye. Like it or not, I miss that baby."

Tim asked, "Just gone? Gone out of town?"

"That's what's so strange. I'm in town doing shopping and sure enough there the two of them are. Only now, Tabatha has to be about ten years old. I greeted them. They seemed very cordial but a bit in a hurry."

"Ann was working somewhere else, then?"

"Yeah, at another bar at the other end of town."

"Do you know where the other place is?"

"Yeah, I believe it was called the Horseshoe."

"Is she still there?"

"My gut feeling is they've left that place already."

Tim and Anita quickly checked out the Horseshoe.

"Sorry, don't know who you are talking about. No nothing, never heard of them and never saw anyone."

It was a no go and another visit with the Police Department Investigation unit proved that they had slipped out of town.

"Now what Tim?"

"The good part is we have a name of a woman with a baby who could fit the description of your Tabatha."

"Can we find out from the train station if anyone like them had left that way?"

"Who knows if they even left by train? More than likely they'd go by car. Easier to stop anyone from tracking them down. They'd be able to get away faster."

"True. What about a car purchase?"

"You still have that picture you drew? Too bad we couldn't get a copy of their mug shot."

"Problem with that is we are doing the work of the cops and I don't think they'll like that."

"Still if we catch up to them, we have to involve them."

"We'll do that when we get closer and it gets dangerous. For now, we have to go looking."

Together they did an intense search of car lots but no one could remember. It had to be the man with the scar for anyone to remember. The others only mattered as to how many were together. This time it would have had to include a lady and a young child.

It was another day and another car lot, "I'd never forget that face. Who drew this picture of this man?"

"I did."

"That's a very good likeness of the man I sold a jeep. He bought the car with cash. He did have a side-kick with him and George called him Sam."

"Where were they going, did the say?"

"George didn't say but Sam mentioned it was going to be a long ride to Chicago with a woman and a child in that vehicle."

"George's last name, do you have it?"

"Let me call Zack."

"Zack, meet these two people, you said your names were?"

"My name is Tim and this is my wife Anita."

"Zack, look at this picture. Didn't I sell that jeep to them?"

"You did."

"Remember the guy's name?"

"You can't give that information to just anyone."

Anita started, "We aren't just anyone. He has my daughter with him."

"What? Have you notified the cops?"

"We have but they haven't been able to find them yet."

"He paid cash for it."

Tim insisted on knowing the license plate number on the jeep.

"Since we aren't a real car dealer, sometimes people can't pay a bill so they leave their car. In this case, the guy that left that car died. He did sign off the title when he gave us the vehicle. George said he would pay his own taxes when he would change the title. If he does or doesn't make the title change is of little consequence to me."

"That's just not so," insisted Zack. "He's using a dead man's name on the title but what would he care. That's how he gets away unknown."

The owner continued, "Not so good but that's how it is. Like I said, we're not a used car dealer, just a repair garage."

Chapter Twenty
Searching Chicago

It was a restless night for Anita with too much to digest knowing they would soon be traveling to Chicago in search of Tabatha. Would it be too late? She was no longer a baby. Up to this point, it had already been another five years later. Now at least fifteen years had passed and she would be a teenager. If there were to be a reunion, would she want any part of it? Why should she, the only mother she ever knew was Ann. What kind of a woman was Ann? Surely she must be one of the gang or how could she still be with George and Sam? They had to have been running from the law with Tabatha in tow.

"Oh, Tim, my head is going to explode. Do you think by now she will have joined up with the gang?"

"Anita, you have to give that to God. He is the only one who knows that answer. We'll find her and then we will know."

"The first thing I'd like to do is find a church to get married in. How about that?"

"I'd love that. Tim, are you really sure you want to marry me with all this baggage?"

"There is no doubt in my mind. It isn't only because we are on this hunt to find your daughter, but when I saw how hard you worked for your keep at the Shelter and then the care you gave each one of the women and children, I decided you were the one for me. Your actions were your testimony as to what God had done for you. My heart told me I didn't want to lose you. I knew then that we could serve together. Even if you didn't love me, I would still have asked you to serve with me at the Shelter. You have to know I'm in love with you and I really do want to marry you even if you want to do other things in other places. I still love you."

Anita gazed in Tim's eyes. "I do love you Tim and let's get married. The future? God, you and I have to figure that out, the three of us."

They found the church and now they were Mr. and Mrs. The honeymoon would wait as they made plans to travel across country to Chicago.

"We need to notify Officer Jim. He'll want to know what we discovered."

They were sitting in the inner office at the Police Station waiting once again.

"Tim, I'm getting restless, I want to go before something really goes wrong."

"We need to be still. If the law is aware of what we know, then by the time we get to Chicago, maybe most of it will have some kind of conclusion or at least we'll know what we have to do next. If we do it alone, our lives will be in danger and then it won't be only us but Tabatha. She'll never get out of that situation if we don't play it right."

"Oh, there he is."

Officer Jim ushered them into his office. "What have you found out?"

"We started with the bar scene because of Anita's prior experience. The first couple of bars proved useless. Finally, we found a Mexican flavored bar. Then it wasn't long and things began popping. Here's what we came up with."

They went into great detail as to how they found the corner garage that was in the back lot with numerous parked cars. "We said, just maybe, let's try this place."

"I didn't have a copy of their picture so I drew it on a napkin at the bar. Somehow, they saw the resemblance."

"Let me see that. You're incredible. If you ever want a job, come see me. You could help us solve a lot of cases."

Officer Jim continued. "With all that info, I'm going to contact Chicago's drug department and when you get there you will need to talk with Sergeant Smith. From the information you gave us Anita, George will be doing his business in pushing drugs."

"Okay, with the conversation we had before, we need to have some guarantee if Anita should get caught in this mix. You know from experience already. She will become his next alibi."

"There isn't a case against Anita, even if she was accused."

"If you have two against one? Both George and this guy Sam? What about the other guy Bill, if he wants to join in?"

"I say it again, there still is no evidence."

"I'll bet my bottom dollar that Sam and Bill have been using blackmail for all of his acquaintances to be a part of his gang."

"That's what we're all hoping. If the others fall off and don't stand by George, we have our man."

"For your encouragement, there is a program called Witness Security Program often called WISTSEC. Designed to protect the witnesses before, during, and after a trial. Families typically get new identities with authentic documentation. It provides job training and employment assistance. A witness who agrees to testify for the prosecution is generally eligible to join the program but it is voluntary. Witnesses are permitted to leave the program and return to their original identities at any time, but once they've entered the program we discourage going back to your original identity."

"I'm assuming Anita would only need that when the trial would come up."

"That's correct."

"She's already changed her surname to mine, so who knows."

"What you never really know is how well George is connected and then with whom. Is he going this alone? To law enforcement it appears bigger than just George, Sam and Bill. It has to be. We already know he's importing drugs at least from Mexico. He has to have contacts much further. They have to have a contact list that we'd like to get. Someone he knows and probably Bill has that information in his possession so that George doesn't get caught with it."

"Is there any way you can direct us to what part of Chicago we could look in?"

"Without anything but mug shots, I don't know."

"We have the vehicle license number of the Jeep. Apparently, the jeep was in the name of a man who had died. If George doesn't re register it, there you have it."

"You have that?"

"We do."

"While you are here, let me have that checked out." Officer Jim was gone for some time. Finally, he came back. His countenance changed. He paused.

"What's wrong?"

"Nothing, I don't think I can let you go there. The downtown part in certain areas is infested with drugs. You can't be a part of that. You could get yourselves killed. Don't go."

"You don't understand. You're talking about my daughter, you can't say no. I have to find her and I don't care that it has been many years that have passed by. I have to go with or without your permission and even with or without Tim. I have to go."

"How about we do it this way, officer Jim. We go up there and check out the schools to see where she is registered?"

"We don't have last names."

Anita was insistent. "We have eyes and ears. At one of the bars Ann worked at, the owner said they called her daughter Tabatha. I'm going to find her."

Officer Jim stopped and looked at Anita. "What did you say? Did you say she is being taken care of by Ann?"

"That's what the guy said."

"Okay, that means Ann Booster is taking care of her."

"You know Ann?"

"We do. So now we know it is George, Sam, Bill and Ann. That gives us a good lead. This is really too dangerous for you to pursue. Can't let you do that."

"Officer Jim, you already know we're going with or without your permission. If you could give us a contact person or shall we report the progress back to you?"

Chapter Twenty-One
Drug Bust

Winter was about to relent its hold against the spring thaw. People trudged down the sidewalk past patches of dirty snow lying in spots on the ground reluctantly giving way to spring flowers here and there. The brown tree trunks stuck out everywhere with bare branches not yet adorned with leaves, outlining the city streets everywhere. Looking carefully, tiny buds could be seen dotting the seemingly dead branches. It wouldn't be long for the green grass to show through in this cosmopolitan city of Chicago even though the crispness was evident in the air.

The sun was disappearing behind the clouds as the sky bathed in the dusk of the evening. The air was placid enough for the sunset to sketch a picture of a dilapidated house, where at the moment, nothing was stirring. The ground was muddied with blotches of snow melting into the weeds. Was the house abandoned? Couldn't be.

An unmarked black Patrol Van with heavily tinted windows was parked directly across with full view of the house. It had a dealer's paper plate covering the regular vehicle license. That was done so that if anyone was to do an illegal run on the plates, they couldn't see the real numbers. There was a scattering of vehicles parked here and there, though sparsely. Nearby, unmarked police cars were parked awaiting the signal call to action.

"Did we bring enough grub for the three of us, Steve?"

"Should be, Bruce. We brought an abundance of bottled water as well."

"We have what we need in the back of the Van should you guys have any needs in the next few hours." Sergeant Smith had been on *stakeouts* before but Steve had special training for this and was licensed to have a canine assistant.

Steve had his eyes glued to watch every move with Atlas sitting beside him. Bruce and Sergeant Smith were armed and ready to jump at the opportune moment should the exact situation unfold, although, they would probably use backup for the action. They were certain they were in the right spot at the right time. An anonymous informer had indicated the exact time they should be there.

The city block was dotted with tiny little bungalows between brick factories. At one time it had been a quiet village were families enjoyed their homes surrounded by white picket fences but that was in their glory days. The neighborhood had shifted when the area was rezoned for businesses. Older people had died, other home owners had no relatives to inherit the land. The others moved farther into the suburbs. The house that was on the *watch* list was a one story-shack that had been abandoned for quite some time.

Neighbors still living in the area had complained for months that there was evidence of drug dealing in the area. During the day light hours there was never any activity but during the night it would be a busy little house. Cars would come and go. Some luxury cars could be seen pulling up and others were clunkers hardly making it up the driveway.

The sun had set, making it pure dark now. Only the streetlights lit the frame of the house. The cops had been waiting for hours. Steve continued to look in every direction, "Think we missed our timing, guys?"

"Ah, why don't you have another sandwich and keep watching. Who knows when the time will be right? Who got the tip for this drug bust anyhow? Does anyone know?"

"It came in earlier in the day, Bruce. We were told that a large amount of *crack cocaine* was being delivered to this vacant run down shack at the end of Elm Street. That's why we are here."

"Maybe our informer was wrong or maybe this wasn't one of those nights and the house is really abandoned." Bruce didn't speak with any certainty.

Smith told them, "Actually, whoever is the informer, told one of the *stoolies* who told one of our guys. We don't know the real source since we aren't permitted to know who the *stoolies* are unless it becomes a life and death situation."

"Better that way." Bruce preferred the anonymity. "Less people get hurt that way when it comes through the department. Less chance of tracing the source."

"That would be good for a reporter. Can't be forced to reveal what you don't know."

It was serenely quiet but only a brief moment now, when unexpectedly before Steve's eyes, all began unfolding.

Steve whispered, "Look!"

Bruce said, "This is payday!"

Street lights made it possible to just barely see black shadows silhouetting the horizon. A couple of men had just stepped out of an old dull-gray Beretta. They walked quickly toward the doorway. It took only minutes for an obvious exchange to take place that should've gone unnoticed.

"Steve did you see them?"

"I did and I noted it on the log."

"Do that later, Steve, call backup." The intensity of the situation was evident when Smith began giving out the orders.

Though everyone was about to pounce on the *drug pushers*, Smith's mind was yet on another house, only a few houses away hid next to an industrial building but he had to let that go as they focused their binoculars on a man with a FedEx box full of something, aware there were no FedEx vehicles in the area.

"Let's call them, Steve. Get the cops to take over!"

"Go get 'em men!" were Sergeant's only words.

The man quickly handed the box over to another making the money exchange but as he was about to make a run for it, unfortunate for him, the cops appeared as though from nowhere. They pounced on him from behind.

Blue and red lights flashed intensely with overwhelming sirens belching out the all too familiar sounds that preceded an emergency. The screeching sirens were deafeningly, almost too close for their ears.

"That is loud," Sergeant Smith wasn't thrilled with what was presenting itself before them. "Another drug bust."

For Steve, this was a successful arrest and more drugs were now off the street. Of course, that wasn't the end of the story for there would be more. Smith, Bruce and Steve were now more concerned with the other house on their watch list.

The three men were done for the evening as they sat in the local coffee shop debriefing their minds and thoughts about everything that just occurred. Smith opened his satchel, pulling out a folder. There wasn't to be a break for the men. Days off, just maybe but their work wasn't about to end tonight. The next case was more like a life and death situation that had to be carefully worked over.

Chapter Twenty-Two
Investigation

"I don't like this one. I know we detest drug busts of any sort but this one is still eluding us."

"Those guys are a cunning bunch." Steve nodded, "This time, we have evidence, Smith."

"You mean, because it says a couple of guys bought the house in cash? It isn't much of a house. Did you see it? The grass is overgrown in the back with nothing but weeds everywhere. We checked the public records for the floor plan. It was once a luxury home but had been abandoned for too many years. The plans showed an attic with a room that had an adjoining bathroom and then a few more rooms on the lower level. With the condition being what it was, it couldn't have cost much. Almost anyone could pay cash for that." Smith was certain of that.

"Still it's a house on a piece of land. Forget the house, the land by itself is worth a good bit of money. It had to be drug money." Steve was confident.

"The land might be worth something but they bought it off the county which means it went up for auction. The cost would have been negligible."

"Even so, it was all cash. Were they checked out when it was acquired?"

"According to the records, it was all legit. Let's surmise that it is drug money, can we prove it?" asked Smith.

"We know it."

"But, can we prove it? We can't assume anything."

Sergeant Smith was in his mid-forties, all of his six feet, husky a man who religiously worked out. He was a man that could think logically in the midst of the battle, a much-needed asset for a police Sergeant and investigator. Everyone knew him to be caring and as he often said, he wasn't just there to carry out everything to the letter-of-the-law. Surely, the law was important in his line of business, how people were dealt with was almost more important to him.

"We need to do an under-cover *stakeout* but this time we need a *stoolie*." Steve liked doing *stakeouts*.

"Who's the *stoolie* to be?" asked Smith.

"Stool pigeon? Me."

"But how, Bruce?"

Steve insisted, "Let's just do another *stakeout*, like the one we just did. It went well enough and if it doesn't go as easy we always have Atlas with us. They deal and we nab them. Drugs are drugs. Make me your *stoolie* and I'll go in just like another druggie. I'll get them. It can't be that hard, dangerous maybe, but not hard."

Steve Burney hadn't gotten over being a Rookie but he enjoyed the *stakeout* scene. He liked being in on the bust. However, he tended to think in *black and white* and sometimes that could be a detriment. He had a medium build with muscles that were evident. His blond hair and blue eyes made him stand out which could work for or against him depending on the people around him.

Bruce Nichols, on the other hand, had the appearance of a wrestler, though not tall either, about 5 feet 10, curly black hair with dark eyes, young and playful looking.

"There is a good reason we can't just do a *stakeout*." Bruce wasn't sure how much his boss and Steve already knew. "I don't know if Steve knows. You would probably know that we have a young lady to contend with here."

"I do, but how did you come across that info?"

"She and a friend of mine attend a small community Church. The house she lives in is the one we've known for a while where drugs are passing through. Just so I could know whom we were working with, I attended the Church with my friend. I wanted the young lady to see me, to avoid the surprise factor. Hopefully she won't want to ignore me should I be the *stoolie*."

Smith continued, "Here, both of you need a copy of this file. There's more to that story. She could easily have been kidnapped or abducted and doesn't know it."

"What?" Steve was alarmed.

"That's what I said." Smith added, "We were starting the investigation process and discovered a young blonde girl was living there. She is about 5 foot 3 inches tall, slender and attends Melville High. We've tracked her to attending that local Community Church on Sundays, the one you already investigated, Bruce. Doesn't do much more than attend. No real involvement and keeps to herself."

Steve tended to go by the book, "We can't take any chances, she would be too important so why aren't we arresting the parents and bringing in Child Protective Services? The young lady surely could do better if she was out of that place."

All but ignoring Steve's comment, Smith continued, "With what we know, there is no evidence that the young lady was ever Ann Booster's or Bill Thomas's daughter. Yet, they are the assumed parents according to the school registry. We checked with the school she attends and the girl goes by the name of Tabatha Rosander. However, we can't find Tabatha anywhere in the public records."

"That is odd, she doesn't even use either of their names."

"All the more reason we should call in CPS and find out who she really is."

"If we do that, Steve, the drug dealers scatter and we never catch any of them and in the process Tabatha could easily get hurt. She's expendable. They only need her presence for them to appear to be legit, law-abiding citizens. When push comes to shove, she's gone and no one would be the wiser for it. She never existed as far as they are concerned."

"But if she was out of that home, she would be safe." Steve insisted.

"Not so, all would be quiet for a time until they came looking and you know they would find her. We can only keep our surveillance on her for so long."

"So then, Smith, it's very possible that even Tabatha wouldn't know who she really is."

"You are right, Bruce."

"We've learned recently from another case where a young girl was lured into running away with a more mature man and then abandoned to other people. That girl was supposed to be sold into prostitution. Fortunately, the young lady panicked. She did have a cell phone with her and called for help. The people she was with played it cool and let her go. Didn't make an issue of it and acted as if they knew nothing. She made it back home safe and sound but not everyone one is so fortunate."

"Smith, I think you better let me handle this. I have a plan."

"I'm listening."

Chapter Twenty-Three
The Idea Man

"This is my idea."

"I become a student at Melville High."

"You think you can pull that off? It's late in the year already."

Steve shook his head. "I still think my way could be safer for us. Besides it'll be months before we solve the case if we do what Bruce wants."

Smith seemed annoyed. "It may take time, but we could save a life. I'd prefer that to having a gun battle. You also need to know, if Bruce is to pull this off, Steve, we'll need you to help us. Eventually we will be doing a *stakeout*, just what you were trained to do." Smith continued, "If this plan of yours, Bruce, is to be the way we need to proceed, we have to pour over all the information we can get. Check with Melville High. Get yourself registered as a student."

Bruce added, "It's a senior high, so that's good. It should be a *slam-dunk* to be passed off as a student without anyone knowing. It will be imperative that not even Melville High can know anything. Only the applicable senior supervisors that dictate to that school, can know."

"We also have to work on the drug gang that go in and out of that house." Smith knew how it had to go. "We do have *stoolies* for that, but we need to know all their details and who everyone is."

"Bug the house?" asked Steve.

"Need a search warrant for that. That's hard to get considering everyone has a legal right to their own personal privacy."

"Even with due cause?" asked Steve

"We don't want to risk having it thrown out of court because we invaded their personal privacy even when we have due cause. It gets pretty tricky so I'd prefer a solid clean case. Let's not forget, there is someone whom we have to protect. We have to find our way into that setup."

Plans began to be conceived. Arrangements had to be made with the district to allow such a process to take place. There would be plenty of red tape and that wouldn't be the only problem. It wasn't going to be easy.

The next day found Sergeant Smith and Bruce Nichols at the Superintendent of Schools office. They identified themselves and shared with Dr. Phil Roberts what they had in mind.

Dr. Roberts wasn't too thrilled with the idea of doing an investigation within the high school.

"What if it comes to playing *cops and robbers?* I could have to end up with a *lock down.* Then we would need to notify the parents that their children would likely be in danger."

"We would never do anything on School property. You have my word on that. We only want one of your students under surveillance to protect her rather than taking her out of the school system."

"I'm not sure about what you are asking. I'm supposed to guarantee the safety for each of my students by whatever means I have available to me. The most I can do is present your request to the school board and see if they want to give permission."

"Can't allow you to do that. This has to be completely confidential. No one can know. Here is the court order," Sergeant presented the paper, "you must allow us to conduct the surveillance."

"I take it, this is no longer in my hands, correct?" The Superintendent had a surprised look. "How can you do this to me?" He intently read and reread the court papers. "No longer in my hands."

"You've got it. We are not intentionally going beyond your authority but this is a very urgent case. We need to protect and serve."

Smith insisted, "There are some needs we want you to assist us in but we will inform you of those as they come up."

"Needs? How can I do more than allow you to invade Melville High?"

"We could need assembly time? Or maybe we will ask for early dismissal of classes? That can't be too difficult."

The Superintendent was obviously disgusted. He had always made it a priority to be sure his students where safe. Most requests he was able to deny, but a court order?

It was arranged. The surveillance was about to begin with Bruce registering as a student.

Bruce made his way to the registrar's office to do a late registration. "Aren't you a little late in the school year?" asked the registrar.

"Sorry, Ma'am, I have to go where my parents go. I take what I can get." Ms. Chatter handed him the paperwork. "I hear good reports about Melville High."

"Wonderful, that's good to hear. I know our school rates first in a lot of categories. Our Art students are some of the best in the Nation. We do competitions from time to time."

"How is the sports program?"

"It's also up there."

"Any classes for wrestling?"

"Yes, I can see you would make a good contender. Would be good for our school to have the winning team. You need to work at that."

"Who would I have to see?"

"Our Superintendent?"

Bruce gave a sigh, "We'll see if I can squeeze it in."

"Don't tell me you've already met him?"

Bruce couldn't let on that he'd just come from seeing him. "He's a good man. It appears from what I hear he always, without failure, makes the students his first priority. He doesn't want anything to happen that might upset his staff or his students."

"I'm amazed that you have garnered that information so quickly. When did you get into town?" Bruce appeared to have a blank look on his face.

"You are new here, right? Otherwise you'd have been registered already."

"That's what I said." He knew he needed an excuse. "My parents are well connected."

"Political people?"

"Not exactly, they're law enforcement."

"Ah, that would make sense. Then, where are you from?"

The questions were coming too quick and he wasn't about to reveal his disguise. "Let me complete the paperwork and you'll see some of my history there. It shouldn't take but a minute to complete this."

"Somehow you interest me. You'll enjoy our school, I'm sure. We get some of the highest grades academically in the State. We're grateful for that."

Bruce handed the paperwork back to the registrar. She hesitated, "I need some kind of identification and where to send for your past information."

"Send it to this address. It is a local address but they will give you everything you need."

Bruce caught up with Sergeant Smith. "Okay, I'm registered but they want all this further information. I gave them what they want in care of you. If you can sit on it as long as I'm working on this case or get it approved with the superintendent of schools."

"Unless I have to, we'll stall. If push comes to shove, we'll get their stamp of approval. See how that goes for now."

Bruce was registered, but now what? He needed to make another appearance at the Church Tabatha was attending and observe her surroundings. He had to know whatever he could to connect with her. See what he could gleam from that. At least she would have seen him visibly more than once and hopefully learn to trust him as a fellow student.

It was a very small Church that supposedly in that past had merely been a chapel for weddings. A Christian group took over the building and began a thriving outreach program making it a very active church. Checking the roster of activities, he could see how a young person could be involved very easily. Bruce decided he would attend church the next day, Sunday. There was Tabatha, the blonde girl. He made sure she had seen him and now he would try to catch up with her at school. It seemed obvious that she was a loner. For now, the fact that Tabatha had seen him without any kind of communication was enough.

The house on the watch list was only a couple of blocks from the church. He exited with other people leaving the church, deliberately passing by the house at a distance without making any obvious connections. All seemed quiet.

Bruce had to remember his position he was playing in this case. He had to scout out the land, make notes on everything. Keep good records that could be followed.

Chapter Twenty-Four
Melville High

"Hey, Hey, girl!"

Tabatha stood still, frozen for the moment. Being careful had become second nature to her. Not for a moment would she allow herself to be taken by surprise. Who was this person anyhow? What would he want from her? Who did this guy think he was anyhow? Everyone had to be a suspect of something.

"Don't try anything with me."

"Oh, no, my name is Bruce. I recently moved into the area and just registered for class."

"A little late in the year, don't you think?"

"I take what I get. When my family moves, somehow I get to go with them whether I'm prepared for it or not. Still another two semesters, what'd I miss? Just the first half maybe?"

"Transfer from another school?"

"Yeah."

"I guess I just have to have my *ducks in a row*, so I try to do everything on time. Though, I'm beginning to rethink that."

"Why would that be? Your family planning on leaving?"

"Don't ask."

"I've seen you around and I think you're in some of my classes. Am I right?"

"Yeah, I remember you and didn't I see you at church Sunday?"

"You did."

"I'm Tabatha."

"That's a neat church you attend. But I don't see you often at the youth functions, actually, I've never seen you at any."

"Yeah, well, it gets too complicated to explain all that to my Mom and Bill, or sorry, my parents so I just do the early morning youth class and then church. They don't ask any questions so it works for me. Until I turn 16, that's good enough for me."

"So when is that delightful event?"

"The end of this school year, when I'm supposed to graduate."

"You started school early or just a smart gal?"

"I guess bit of both but I don't know about the *smart* stuff. I'm not that far ahead of everyone. Maybe a bit ahead for my age."

"Like I said, a humble but smart gal."

"I can hardly wait to go it on my own."

"I know the feeling. There's so much I want to do when school gets out. Places to be. Get on with my own life." Bruce carefully looked at Tabatha. "For you, why would you be so eager to leave?"

"Just what I need to do. For me it will be the right thing to do."

"Do you hang with other kids? I'm sure you must."

"I try not to."

"Your reasoning for that?"

"I wouldn't want to reciprocate."

"I'm sure you are well liked."

"I wouldn't want to give it a chance. Like I said, it won't be long and I'll be out of here."

"But, the fun you miss by not mixing."

"Why would I be telling you, anyhow?"

"Like you said, I've had a late start at Melville. At least you could be my friend, I need a friend, right about now."

"You? Why should you need a friend?"

"Same reason as you?"

"That's impossible, no one lives like me. There isn't another person in all the world, believe me."

"Can't be so, Tabatha. There is always someone else in similar circumstances, like maybe me. Other kids have problems probably the same as yours and could use a friend like you."

"I don't really have any personal problems, just stuff that seems to happen around the house. I'm not about to involve people in my family. Taking care of myself is quite enough for me."

"How long have you lived where you are now?"

"We've lived at this house my whole senior year but why don't we just talk about other things? Besides, I need to go soon. What did you say your name was?"

"Yeah, my name is Bruce. See you in class? What time do you get to school?"

"Have to go." Tabatha didn't answer his questions.

Tabatha was off. She felt she had said enough to a total stranger. She wasn't sure she wanted to get involved in something she couldn't handle. Besides, who was Bruce anyhow? Just the best looking kid in school and he was talking to her? Why?

She was returning to a home she was longing to abandon. In her mind, when school would let out, it wouldn't be soon enough. Maybe she should devise a plan, but how?

Could she get away with leaving at age 16? *I'm surely going to try. When I'm faced with what I have to do, I'll know how to handle it. Something has to give. I can't keep clinging to Mom's apron strings to stay safe and I'm almost an adult, anyhow.*

It was now a different day and surely enough, who should be walking toward the School? Both of them were coming from different directions yet somehow they were now facing one another.

"Well, well, like you said, here we are. May I escort you to class?"

"I don't need an escort, Bruce."

"Do you mind if we walk in together, though?"

"No, I don't mind."

"What's your first class?"

"Literature."

"Strange."

"Why?"

"You are beginning to scare me, Tabatha, that's my class. Mrs. Brown seems to be a good teacher. Don't you think? I kind of like her because she makes a lot of sense and thinks logically. I like logic."

"You mean, like in order? *Ducks in a ...*"

"*Row, Ducks in a Row.* Easier to decipher, don't you think?"

"Maybe my next class will stump you, Bruce. It's on World Politics. None of that makes a lot of sense but I guess we have to know that too."

"I guess, Tabatha."

"Don't tell me, you're in that class too?"

"I am. Those might be the only two."

"That's just 'cause then I'm taking a music class. I don't know why, though."

"Sounds like a fun class. What instrument do you play?"

"The flute, it's hard to play but I love it. The biggest problem is the only practice I get is after school with the school's instrument and then only for a very short time."

"Usually the school allows your parents to rent them during the year. If you do well you can buy it for a lot less at the end of the year."

"That would be the day that I could get to keep the flute."

"I'll bet it is good for your mind, though. Love to hear you play sometime."

"Don't know about that but it does keep me sane, I think."

That was class and then everyone separated. Bruce didn't want to be too nosey. He knew he had to play it cool. He needed to be especially careful and not allow his heart to get in the way of the original plan. He must deflate that idea immediately. There was no place for getting involved personally. That was not what he had signed up for. This was purely an investigation.

Chapter Twenty-Five
Coffee

Bruce and Smith met up at the local coffee shop to share information. Smith was getting concerned. "It's been a couple of weeks. How are we coming with your information on Tabatha?"

"I'm trying to ease in on her. She wants to be a closed book. She is afraid to talk."

"Come on, Bruce you're a handsome young man, throw some charm her way. That's the least you can do for her."

"You don't get it, Smith, that's exactly my biggest problem."

"You want to like her."

"I already do. Think about it, I'm going to betray her."

"Don't go there, Bruce, you can't think of it that way. You have to realize this is all about saving her life. Remember that and may I repeat, *you are going to save her life*."

"Her confidence, I'm going to betray her confidence, Smith. Can I do that? I've always been a *straight arrow*. Now I have to betray the most innocent person I ever had to work with and I'm beginning to get feelings for her."

Smith wouldn't leave it alone. "Let me try. Just play the *straight arrow*. You would have to tell her why you want to get to know her. Tell her to spill her guts to you and trust that you don't destroy the rest of her life. She's a teenager. Teenagers live in the crisis of the moment. To them, their world feels like it is going to be over. You must know that none of what you say to her is going to make sense. Her biggest dilemma will be, *whom can she trust?* Take it from me. At that age we run and where would she run? She knows very well her *home life* is no place for refuge. She has no one to ask for advice. She's surviving until she can live on her own. Believe me, she'll run because she no longer has anything to lose. Do you think she'll understand that?"

"I guess not, too dangerous. She already told me, she's planning on running as soon as she turns 16 and that's when school lets out. I'm afraid if that happens without any help, they'll not only find her and very possibly kill her if she is uncooperative. Then think about it, sixteen isn't the age of independence from her parent's care. Not only that, being she attends church, she'll very likely have an acute conscious. Likely that could mean there would be no way she'll get involved in their drugs. You and I know that they'll demand she does. That won't be the worst of it. They'll want to put her in their prostitution ring."

"Remember it was your idea to get involved like this. I liked your idea and now you have to make it work. It'll never work with anyone else. You are the man."

"If I'm the man, let's work out a useable plan."

"Work on the information we are going to need. See if she will tell you about herself. Where is she from and what does she know?"

"I'll try for the info first."

"We need to know her birthdate for when she turns 16. Try to find out all the places they moved from. Don't believe those guys would stay too long anywhere. We have to act before she has her sixteenth birthday so that she doesn't get into any trouble we can't handle."

"Possibly, if I can get something of hers to get a DNA testing, do you think?"

"That's good, try to see if you can get something from her. Report that back to me. We have to get on with it. The drug trafficking is very active in that home. We can't delay much longer."

He and the Sergeant parted ways but Bruce sat in his car for a moment to clear his thoughts. *How in the world is a person like me going to get something personal enough from her? No matter how I look at it, I'm walking on dangerous ground.* If he wasn't careful he was going to sink into the desires of his heart. He knew it wouldn't take much. If only he could take her home and away from the circumstances to save her life. Why couldn't he? His head and his common sense told him he couldn't do that though he knew her danger was imminent.

There was a reason for allowing her to continue in her situation. It couldn't merely be to rescue Tabatha with law enforcement involvement but it had become needful for not only did they have an unidentifiable sixteen-year-old in the midst of the drug deals, they had been tipped off that at least one of the men was a killer. To break the *drug ring* would be imperative to solve the case. Bruce had to work through this case step by step. He was determined. *I don't care what is required of me, but if Tabatha faces any dangerous situations, I will rescue her. If she or the Department doesn't like it, so be it!*

It was now time for him to put a leash on the ache in his heart even if that meant going into *remote control*. Maybe if he started to speed up the process, he could keep a bit more disconnected. He knew for certain that was not going to be easy. How could he not fall in love with such a beautiful girl? He wasn't that much older than her. What, eight or nine years? What if she didn't like that? Bruce shook his head. *What am I thinking about? I need to go to the gym and work out.* He did just that.

Bruce hadn't planned on meeting anyone at the gym, he just wanted to clear his head.

"Hey, Buddy, what brings you here this time of day?"

"Pastor, surprised to see you." Bruce continued, "Time to force myself into thinking straight. What's up with you, Pastor Dave?"

"Not a thing, Bruce, you working on a case?"

"That I am. My heart keeps getting in the way."

"Hey Buddy, why don't you tell me about the girl you are falling in love with?"

"Can't do that but I need a level head right about now."

"When it comes to falling in love, I certainly know how that goes."

They spent the afternoon working on building muscles.

"I've had it for today, Bruce. Have to call it quits for now. How about you?"

"Yeah, I guess I will too. I think I worked out the cobwebs for now. Whether I like it or not, it will take more than just a little bit of time."

"Sounds like a big one. Have you asked God for help?"

"I have. It will take Him to work it through to the end. Funny, I know that but my heart insists on getting in the way."

"Wish you well. If you want to talk sometime, let me know, I'm listening. See you later." Pastor Dave was gone.

Bruce wasn't about to share the dilemma that concerned a parishioner of Pastor Dave's.

Chapter Twenty-Six
On The Grounds

    A week had rolled by and no matter how hard Bruce attempted to get answers from Tabatha she wasn't sharing much of anything with him. Going slow didn't appear to give him the necessary answers he had to have. It wouldn't be long before he would have to insist on more information. He knew very well, if it came to that, everything would end up hitting the *fan*. His source for answers would be over and he may very well have lost a life in the process.

    Today was a nice sunny but windy day in Chicago. Common for this time of year, though warm by Illinois standards.

    The two met yet again, Bruce and Tabatha.

    "How did you do on that homework assignment, Tabatha?"

    "Hard."

    "I'm surprise, an intelligent person like you? What's up? Maybe I can help you."

    "You can't change my circumstances."

    "Can't be long now, Tabatha. You are a senior at Melville. When do you turn 16?"

    "On the 27th of May, almost the end of May when I finally turn 16. Just about when school is out. My problem is I want to graduate. I want to have that diploma. Maybe someday I can go to College."

    "Let me help you with your homework. We have a few minutes before class. Here, let me see what you've done." Bruce thumbed through the paperwork with great interest. He couldn't let on that he wasn't really a student and he couldn't afford to become a teacher to her.

"You've done it all, better stuff than what I did. Let me put your papers in order. There, that should do it. I'm certain you are better in this subject than I am. You are a very brilliant kid, Tabatha."

"I don't know how I did that. I really tried but it seemed impossible so I just quickly threw everything together and ran out the door as quickly as I could."

"Why was that?"

"Don't know, but it's always the same. Very noisy all night, and I'm supposed to sleep?" Tabatha was quiet for the moment.

"Anything going on? Does that happen all the time?"

"Very often but somehow last night I couldn't just sleep through like I usually do. Somebody wanted to fight. Luckily it was only a shouting match."

"Are you saying, your mother and father had a fight?"

"Oh, no, not them, they never fight with each other. Other men came and went for most of the night. Usually they just do whatever it is they do and by morning all is quiet. This time it was some guys that came visiting who started a fight."

"You've never told me what kind of work your dad does."

"Have no idea, but believe me, it isn't long now before I'm getting out of there."

"Where do you suppose you are going when you leave home, anything in mind?"

"Darned if I know. I just have to go. I've thought about living at the Y. The security is supposed to be good there."

"You surprise me. You'd leave your family behind?"

"For a time, at least until I could begin to make sense of everything. I'd only be leaving my mother behind. Bill isn't really my dad anyhow."

"Sorry, didn't know that."

"Mom used to say that Bill was a *make believe father.*"

"So, am I correct that Bill is your step dad?"

"Mother is all I've ever known. She and Bill aren't married. That goes over big at church but I don't think the Pastor even knows that."

"But is sixteen the legal age in Illinois?"

"If I was going to College I could pull that off. Mom would easily agree to that."

"I didn't mean to be probing for information. You're my kind of gal, though. A mind of your own and you know where you want to get with your life in the future. I have always admired that in a person."

"We've got to be getting to class."

Bruce tried his best to appear to be unconcerned about anything other than what was on the agenda in class. He had to be careful. He couldn't allow himself to be obvious as to his purpose. Fortunately, most of the classes consisted of lectures and homework assignments. There wasn't much interaction between teacher and students.

They left together after class but Tabatha was obviously exhausted. "I don't know. I need to be going. See you around."

"What did you say, you don't know? Don't know what?"

Tabatha didn't wait. She was gone but Bruce felt at peace with himself, he had laid the groundwork and acquired more information than he had hopped for so quickly.

Tomorrow he would try again, maybe become her buddy. If she wasn't such a pleasant person, he could stay disconnected. His thoughts went deeper than just her appearance and that made it more concerning than he had anticipated. Like he told Sergeant Smith, he cared about her. It had to be his own secret, she couldn't know about his concerns or the reasons.

It would have been easier if he didn't care. If she deserved her surroundings, but in this case, he was almost assured she had no idea who she really was nor did she have any idea she might not even be a daughter to the woman she called her mother. She said, as much, Bill wasn't her father. She'd even leave them behind until she had figured it out for herself.

Bruce had another dilemma. How would he be able to get something for DNA testing? Pull her hair? He hadn't even touched her as of yet. They weren't an item or boy and girl friend at least not as far as she was concerned. Surely he would love to make that attempt, yet even though he started to care he couldn't allow himself that pleasure. He knew he wouldn't be able to stop his feelings and he didn't even know if she would reciprocate. Sergeant Smith had to have a sample for DNA testing very soon for the investigation to have the proof they needed. Time wasn't on their side anymore. He knew the sooner he could get that the closer they would be to solving the mystery of who Tabatha was.

The heartstrings were being pulled, he felt as if he could die. He didn't know how to stop caring for Tabatha.

Chapter Twenty-Seven
Graduation Ceremonies

The very next day, Tabatha and Bruce met yet again on the way to class.

"I hear there is a Dance on Friday. Planning to go? Be my date?"

"I don't think I can do that. I don't have a lot of clothes and stuff. I don't really mind that, but I have even less than nothing. Oh, I'm grateful for what I have, like food and a pair of jeans and some okay clothes but nothing to brag about. Like I said, it's just too complicated."

Tabatha sat cross-legged beside her backpack on the grass tossing her blond curls back over her shoulders. Bruce sat facing her.

"Would you go with me if you had the clothes you think you need?"

"In the first place, that is quite impossible. I haven't the money."

"But I have friends. Might be *hand-me-downs* but they would be the best."

"You mean, my size? I don't believe you, that's totally impossible."

"That just isn't so. I can make it happen."

"After it's all over, how would I unload the clothes? I could never take them home with me."

"I could even arrange that for you."

"What would I tell my Mother? I've never been anywhere. I don't know what she would say."

"Can I come and ask her?"

"Don't like to have people come home with me. My Mom and Bill tend to have their own friends that do things I wouldn't want anyone to experience. Besides, these days, no one wants to visit in a smoke filled room with drunken men. Not nice, just believe me, I know."

"I'm sorry. Are these people you talk about alcoholics?"

"Alcohol I think I could tolerate."

"You're saying your parents do drugs?"

"Like I told you, Bill is not my dad, but he gets drunk most of the time. Mom doesn't. It isn't really them I'm afraid of. It would be the other guys that keep coming around late at night. They do the fighting and I suppose it would have to be about money. What else would people like that fight about?"

"I'd love to have you come visit my family. They wouldn't expect anything and it just might give you the break I'm very sure you need."

"Sorry, couldn't do that. I've never been anywhere. I feel like they keep a *short leash* on me. I haven't ever tried to pull on it to see how far it stretches. It would hurt and I'm really afraid they'll likely lock me up."

"Lock you up? Has that ever happened to you before?"

"No, but they've threatened plenty of times. That was a kind of discipline I've always had to put up with. I've learned to keep my mouth shut, don't say anything to anyone. Mom doesn't threaten me. She'd give me the world if she could. She told me she was going to make some of them pay for my college."

"That's good, isn't it?"

"I wouldn't take a penny from any of those guys. I'd have to pay back with my soul. No way, I have to do this on my own and that's why I have to find a way to leave, I have to find a better way."

"You know they'd never get away with locking you up or doing anything to you. Just give the word and I can solve that problem personally. We'd ... sorry, but the law would be down on them in a minute."

"How would the law find out about me?"

"Let's get real, Tabatha, you told me, right? Going forward, that won't happen. You can depend on it."

"I guess when all is said and done, I really appreciate that. At least you are watching out for me now. Then again, you shouldn't know any of this stuff. I'm going to get in trouble."

"Don't believe that for a minute. Let's talk about the dance. I still want you to be my date. Would you?"

From nowhere, Marybeth popped up. "Hey, Tabatha, what gives? Going to the school dance? There is also a fashion show we can enter and what's more the school plans to hand out scholarships at this event. I wouldn't be surprised if you earned something quite worthwhile."

"You really think so?"

"I do. You work very hard. The rest of us try to have more fun at the expense of our studies. Please, you really have to come."

"Thanks for the vote of confidence but no, Marybeth, I don't think I can. I'm busy."

"How about you, Bruce? Are you coming?"

"Can't. I have other plans."

"I'll bet!" She was being a bit sarcastic. "See you guys." Marybeth was off to see other classmates.

"Come on, Bruce, why don't you go. Why don't you take Marybeth, she'd love that? The best looking guy in our entire school, of course, she would love that. It would be good for her and then she'd probably stop being such a nosey pest all the time."

"No, if I can't take you Tabatha, I wouldn't consider going. Did you know you've become my *soul-mate*?"

"No, I didn't know that." Tabatha wasn't about to let Bruce off the hock. "You have to admit though, Marybeth is kind of cute with her brunette braids and freckled face. From what I've observed, she has to be one of the most lovable gals at Melville High, annoying but lovable."

"Think about what I said. Like you, I have a lot to do when I get home. Since my parents are away a lot, my responsibilities don't stop with schoolwork."

"If I'm your *soul-mate*, what about when we meet?"

"What about church on Sunday?" Bruce wanted to know Tabatha from all sides, and he did enjoy attending church any opportunity he could get. Often he was on duty on Sundays but on this assignment, whatever Tabatha chose to do was his obligation. This was one more piece to the puzzle Bruce had to put together. They parted ways for a day. It would be Saturday and then Sunday when she would see him yet again.

Heading back to her home Tabatha couldn't help but think about the comfort there was in having a friend like Bruce. A kid who wanted nothing more than to be a friend and share a family. If he was for real, he was becoming more than she had ever expected. *He's muscular, good looking. Why would he care about me? Isn't that kind of strange or even odd? It's almost like this isn't where he belongs.* She thought for a bit, *a girl must be careful but studying with him is to my advantage. I'm going with that and only that.*

Together their habit was to meet in the outfield and study for an hour or so. Going over what they had heard in class and digesting important facts they needed to remember, that is, Tabatha had to remember.

I sometimes wonder what has happened here. A kid I've never seen before just shows up and we become soul-mates? How was that even possible? Why would he be interested in me? Yet, he's becoming my lifeline and that scares me. This is not what I'm used to.

Chapter Twenty-Eight
Church

"You made it."

"I did. Come with me. I want to talk with you." They walked to the back of the parking lot. "I still have to ask you. Would you please be my date for the dance?"

"I'm too scared to change my routine. Don't think I can."

"What if I went with you to your house?"

"They won't be nice to you."

"Who won't be nice to me?"

"The guys that come and go, in and out."

"It doesn't matter to me what people say or think. I just want to meet your mother. Maybe, we could get there before *the guys* come."

"Don't know. That's a possibility except that they don't have a schedule. I never know when they come. When I see them come, I run upstairs to my room. Lock the door and hope no one comes looking for me. I don't know."

"Want to try?"

"Let me think. Let's get in Church. Might be a good sermon today. Might just help me."

"Let's."

The message, it seemed as though it was another confirmation for Tabatha. She couldn't help thinking, was the Pastor correct in saying that things could really work out to the glory of God if she was walking in His will and plan for her life? Would God really protect her? Would He allow her a plan of escape? Tabatha knew she had to have a way out of the mess she was living in very soon. There would be no way she could entertain staying around the house after graduation with idle time on her hands. It would not be a good thing with drunk and drugged men coming around every day. She knew the ground beneath her was pretty shaky but if she trusted that her life was in God's hands, wouldn't He provide a way? Maybe Bruce was a Godsend and she should just take it for what it seemed to be. Trust God for her answers.

The service was soon over. The Pastor was at the door to greet his parishioners as both came by and shook his hand.

"Sorry, I didn't know you knew Bruce, Tabatha?"

"From school. We met at school."

"We study together, Pastor."

"You study?"

"Yes, Pastor, Bruce and I study together in the *outfield*. Though I think it is more visiting together. He's a good friend. He said I am his *soulmate*."

"You said that Bruce?"

It was just about all Bruce would need. Would his Pastor blow the investigation cover?

"I did say that. I learn more from Tabatha than I could learn just listening to lectures from teachers. I did say that Tabatha has become my *soulmate*."

"Okay, Bruce." As a Pastor, he knew very well that often Police get caught up in investigations. He would not betray confidences even when he knew little or nothing. Then at the same time as the Shepherd of his flock he needed some answers as well.

"How about a game of golf this week, Bruce?"

"Let's do it pastor. Early morning before the birds catch the worms?"

"Tomorrow."

On the way to Tabatha's house, she asked Bruce, "Why did Pastor question you so much?"

"About me being your *soulmate*? He's just interested in the both of us but I'll ask him tomorrow morning."

"Are you going to make it to class on time?"

"Easy, we'll just have a short game of golf. We won't do the whole course. Besides I like meeting you before class. Gives us a clear head for what we have to face in class, don't you think?"

"How did I do all this before I met you?"

"You did it just fine, but it's a whole lot more fun having someone to talk to for encouragement, don't you think?"

"Yeah, I guess you are right."

"Our Pastor seems to think I'm more of a wrestler than a student. I wouldn't worry about him."

"I didn't know you wrestle?"

"I've done some. There isn't a wrestling team at this school. The registrar thought I should start one."

"Why don't you?"

"Been too busy and it is soon time for graduation."

"I guess."

Tabatha knew she didn't have much time but she would need to get home before someone would wonder about her absence.

"Tabatha, how about I come with you and just see what your mother might say?"

"I don't know. I'm really scared."

"How about if everything goes wrong, I just excuse myself and leave. That way we at least have a plan and just maybe you could do this one outing, the dance. After all, it is a school function. Not like I'm asking you to a nightclub. Then, think about this. If I see that the whole plan won't materialize, I'll just ask them if they would want to be at your coming graduation. Maybe ask your mother to allow you to come with me for plan formulating. Then we still do what you want, however that goes."

"I'm tempted. Maybe just come and I'll introduce you as a friend. Maybe, but I don't know. I just don't know."

Tabatha was in a real quandary. How would she handle all this? Finally, someone who really seemed to care about her and she didn't know how to respond. How could she? This had never happened before. For sixteen years, there was no one but God. Oh sure, there was Ann. She was a good mother who cared for her as well as she could. All her needs had been met over the years. Yet, there was no one to accompany her to school functions or even church. As a child she was dropped off at the church for Sunday school and picked up after the church service was over. Her mother was kept busy working at the local bar twenty-four seven, every day with no exceptions. Nothing ever changed. Now she was about to introduce to her a man she had met at school?

"Want to try?"

"Let me just show you the house."

They walked through the tall brush as they approached the house. "What do you think Bruce? Shabby, wouldn't you say?"

"Please Tabatha, I wouldn't say anything. It doesn't make a bit of difference to me."

"Have to admit it looks pretty unkempt. Look at the weeds everywhere, knee deep. Sometimes I ask my mother if I can clean it up. She just says forget about it. It's how the men want it. She says they like it to look abandoned on the one hand but somehow it's important to have the *family* appearance. Go figure."

"I get the picture. I really do want to meet your mother. Your mother must be a very special person to put up with what must be going on around her. Do you think I can meet her?"

"I don't know Bruce. Let's talk tomorrow." It was all Tabatha could allow for the moment. God would have to work on her but she wasn't going to be brave enough to make introductions. Bruce would have to wait.

"Okay, I understand. See you on the outfield?"

"Sounds good to me, Bruce."

Bruce knew now for certain this was the house under surveillance. He saw the structure, simple and dilapidated. Overgrown underbrush was everywhere. Old cars that had been in obvious car wrecks, counting at least five and if he didn't know better, it looked more like a home for a junk collector. It could only be a place for someone who didn't choose to be a part of the local society. To him, it didn't look habitable much less a place for a person like Tabatha.

Chapter Twenty-Nine
Meetings

"We have to step up the process, Bruce. How goes everything?"

"I almost persuaded her to allow my meeting her mother. I want her to go to the dance with me but she has no clothes to wear. For real."

"We certainly can arrange that."

"I know and I passed it off as though I could get her the best *hand-me-downs* so she wouldn't get wise. She almost accepted that but she still is very afraid to ask her mother. We went to her house where she was going to introduce me. That didn't happen because she was frightened. I can tell you for certain, it is the house we have under surveillance. Not only that, the men that come by the house are definitely into drugs."

"Well, at least that piece of the puzzle is in."

"I want to meet her mother. I have to know where she stands in the scheme of things."

"That's good, we need to know that. We also need to know who's selling and who's buying, where they hide the stuff and what exactly they hide."

Steve insisted, "Wouldn't be too hard Sergeant, to find the stuff once we pounce on them. We can use Atlas to do the finding."

"Not so fast, Steve, Bruce, it is imperative now that you get something for us so we can test her DNA. It takes time to get that information back to us once we send it in."

"A drinking cup? Would that work?"

"Try for a strand of hair."

"That means I have to get her to that dance and that's a hard one."

"If you can pull that off, we'll get more than enough to test."

"How's that?"

"She'll have to change clothing and she could do that at your place."

"Here's my problem, I've already invited her to my place to meet my parents and may I remind you, my parents don't even live here. I did tell her they are usually out of town. I also told her that with my connections I could get the clothing she needs for the dance."

"That was a good excuse, your *parents* being gone most of the time, that could work, Bruce."

"If I can persuade her to pick up the clothes at my place. What if that doesn't happen?"

"Get her to have a cup of coffee at the local coffee shop with you. You can make that happen."

"Suppose."

"Try what you can but time is not on our side anymore."

"Got it Sergeant. But there's one more kink in our plan. I walked out of church with Tabatha. That seemed to concern Pastor."

"Obviously, should've left separately."

"Now I have a golf game with him on Monday morning at 7 am and I don't golf, it doesn't happen to be my game. Of course Tabatha doesn't know that. Then at 7:45 I have to meet Tabatha in the outfield."

"You're a man of great wisdom. You know how to handle Pastor Nelson and you'll know exactly what to tell him so you can keep your obligations."

"I do?"

"Here's another idea, Bruce, I'm going to arrange to have the school out early. It will come from the district since the school doesn't really know what's going. That will get you to the coffee shop and the cup, if you can manage that. The quicker we get that off for testing the better."

"Maybe then you could also get us the half day on Friday to prepare for the dance?"

"If you can get her to go, we'll work that out. The school will probably do that anyhow, but we'll be sure they do."

Now it would be another meeting. This one he didn't look forward to. Bruce knew full well what Nelson's concerns were. Would he be able to share his involvement with Tabatha or would he need to make up an excuse?

The next morning the sun was barely up or was it that Bruce was barely awake? He needed to hurry to meet with Nelson. He couldn't avoid the meeting because if he did the whole incident could be blown apart. There is no way Nelson would allow one of his defenseless parishioners to be accosted when he could have stopped such an event.

"Bruce, I'm glad you could make it."

"I'm sorry, Pastor but I don't know what to tell you."

"Try me."

"I can't go into details, but mostly I'm afraid this could all blow up in my face and then Tabatha's troubles would only have just begun. Why don't you tell me first about what you know about her?"

"Bruce, I'm not in the habit of divulging my people's lives with anyone."

"Okay, I'll accept that. If you know anything about Tabatha, I'm here protect her, as a law enforcement officer. Life is not what it seems for her and I've been assigned to her for her protection. But I cannot for one moment allow her to know. Please, don't rat on me. It is her life I'm protecting."

"I don't know a whole lot but I do look out for the youth of our church especially. Tabatha doesn't say much. When they started coming to this church, Ann introduced herself as her mother. Excused herself that she couldn't attend but would I pray that God would work out their situation. She was more concerned for Tabatha than herself. I invited her to talk with me but that has never happened. I tried on one occasion to visit but was told by a man not to come back. He said there was no one home and they were not interested in the church."

"Tell me, what did that man look like?"

"Dark hair with a definite scar on his face. I'd know him if I ever saw him again."

"Did you get his name?"

"I heard another man in the back ground call him George. Apparently the other name I heard someone mention from in the house, was Sam. They talked back to each other as I stood at the doorway."

"All of that helps. At least we know some names of the people we are dealing with." Bruce glanced down at his watch. "Oh, I have to go. Have to meet Tabatha..."

"I heard, on the outfield. Go with God and I will be praying very intently."

"Thanks."

There was no time to waste. Bruce had to get to the school as quickly as possible but time was moving fast.

Tabatha had been waiting but since Bruce hadn't turned up, she was on her way to the school's front entrance.

"Tabatha!"

"Where have you been? How did the golfing go?"

"Went well enough but I'm not a pro golfer. So here I am, sorry I'm late. Wow, you look tired. What's up?"

"Nothing, just the same, I'm concerned about you wanting to meet my mother. I want to and see if I get a scholarship but other than that, your proposal frightens me."

Lectures went as usual through the day and after the last morning class, a P.A. system announcement came that classes would be dismissed for the day.

It seems we got out earlier today. Must be everyone was tired from last night. I think you need some coffee."

"I think you are right."

"Why don't I treat you to a Frappuccino at the coffee shop."

"I can't be long, though."

"We'll be back at your house just like normal. Now relax."

They sat together enjoying the refreshment. Bruce notice Sergeant Smith was sitting in the corner. *Sure hope he doesn't acknowledge my presence.*

"You know, Bruce, last night Bill came home and must've been so drunk that all I could hear was the sound of bottles flying everywhere. Didn't hear my mother, so he couldn't have touched her but it wasn't more than 15 minutes before he must've passed out. Fortunately for me, my room is in the attic. I even have my own bathroom so it isn't half bad. I guess Ann and Bill, sorry, I mean my Mom and Bill wanted me out of the way so they have always put me up there ever since we first moved there. I'm glad for that, especially because Bill has always had these episodes for as long as I remember. Wouldn't be so bad but it's always about 2:30 in the morning. Seems something goes bad with him and then I hear all that."

"Probably, the bar closes at 2 am. Might be why it's always 2:30 am when he comes home. Were you able to get enough sleep?"

"Yeah, I'll be okay. I don't require a lot. I never thought about the bars closing at that time of night. That explains those late nights. You know what, Bruce, you are just too smart!" Tabatha rested her head in her hands with her elbows propped on the table.

Tabatha was intelligent enough to know it had to be more than just alcohol. She looked up at Bruce, "You suppose they do drugs as well?"

"Drinking and drugs don't mix well. Could be why he has such extreme temper tantrums."

"I know I could report what happens but then what? Where do I go from there? Probably locked up in an institution. I'm too old for a family to care about someone like me and I've worked so very hard on my grades. I don't need to be pulled out of this school right about now. This wouldn't be a good time. Besides, I've heard plenty of horror stories. Most girls like me are picked by people who want to abuse us." Tabatha felt she didn't need any more trials in her life.

Bruce went over to the counter to buy the drinks, purchasing a cup for Tabatha.

"Here Tabatha, this is your very own cup with your drink in it."

"What will I do with that after I've finished? I don't want to take it home."

"That's okay, I'll keep it in my car for the next time we do this. How's that?"

"That'll work, I guess. You know, Bruce, I just really get the feeling that Mom isn't even my mother. I already know Bill is not my father, but my Mother?"

"Why would you say that?"

"Because it's too confusing for me.

"You have a birth certificate, don't you?"

"I'm sure I should."

"It would at least tell you where you were born and what city or State you are from."

"Yeah, maybe, but where would I find it? I've never seen it. No matter what, though, I'm afraid it could be more than just alcohol or drugs Bill is into. A drunk, maybe but when his buddies come around I keep thinking they are up to more than using. That's when I would rather not be near the house."

"Why would you want to be with this Bill and his drunken buddies?"

"I guess that figures. And I don't think Ann is like that either. She just tolerates it." Tabatha turned to face Bruce, "I can't believe I've been sitting here this long. I've got to get out of here. I know my way back. You don't have to drive me. I'm fine."

Bruce reached over Tabatha's shoulder to take the cup and accidentally skimmed his hand past her hair. "Oh, I'm sorry, I didn't mean to pull your hair. Are you okay."

"That didn't hurt but let me take that piece of my hair off the glass."

"Don't worry about that, I'll take care of everything."

Tabatha was gone. Bruce sat there for a moment without moving. Sergeant Smith joined him.

"How did that go?"

"Have a cup I'm keeping for Tabatha and a piece of her hair."

"That was good work, smart move."

"I've seen the house. Not much, just a few car wrecks in the yard. Overgrown grass and mostly weeds. I got to meet her mother at the bar where she works. She recognized me but I played it cool and said we could have met in other places so she let it be. I asked Tabatha about her birth certificate. She's never seen it."

"That could make it very difficult to find out her identity. Keep trying. We'll try the DNA, but that takes time. See what else you can get."

Chapter Thirty
Piece of the Puzzle
———

Bruce hadn't been able to meet Ann yet but he had a few more answers to the puzzle. He now knew two more names, George and Sam.

Still Tabatha couldn't help but think, *this guy is flattering me. Who is Bruce anyhow? Should I run before I can't get out of this situation? It's just too much for me. I think I need to make plans for my future, sooner than later. He's become my soul mate? How could I let that happen? I haven't even taken the time to know anything about him. Okay, he did offer to have me come meet his family. I don't know, I just don't know.*

Tabatha made her way into her house through the side entrance she had always done in the past. The entire house had shingles for the roof and siding as well. Bits of the brown wood color could be seen through the worn black left from the wind and the rain. It was basically a one-bedroom home with an attic. Yet, it had two bathrooms, one next to Tabatha's room in the attic and then one on the main floor for Ann and Bill. Insulation in the house was pathetic considering every word could be heard throughout the entire house.

It was still early afternoon, just after church but she hadn't eaten yet, so she would have to make her way into the tiny kitchen and help her mother with lunch.

Tabatha's mind wouldn't give her any peace. *I just don't get it. What would a guy like Bruce want from me? Surely there are a lot of uncomplicated girls he could rather date. Why had he chosen me? Then he said he was my soul mate. How did that happen? Did I encourage that?*

Tabatha started the dinner with her mother. "Are any of the guys coming over, Mom?"

"I don't expect anyone today. Usually everyone stays away on Sunday." Ann hesitated for a moment. "You know, Tabatha, years ago, my husband and I used to go to church all the time. In fact he was an elder in the church."

"What happened that you don't go anymore?"

"Maybe someday I'll be able to tell you. I just can't today. We should prepare for Bill, though. He'll be hungry when he comes home."

"Do you think you will ever marry Bill, as you called him once, my pretend father?"

"Not on your life! I'm only here because you are my charge."

"Me?"

"I want to make very sure you get your education so that you can go on in life to take care of yourself. You don't need to depend on other people for your everyday needs. Then maybe you will find a decent Christian man and have a life of your own."

"You don't like to work at the Bar?"

"I can't believe I'm doing it. Yet for you and your safety I'll do anything. Walk through hell if I have to."

"Something like, *though I walk through the valley of death, I will fear no evil?* You know Mother, God will take care of me no matter what. If you don't want to work there, I'll bet you could get a better job."

"It's much more complicated than that. I have to deal with George and Sam."

"Why can't you and I just leave? I just want to graduate and then we could do that."

"Sorry, when you leave me, you will be on your own. Don't you dare tell anyone where you are, I don't want them to hunt you down."

"What are you saying?"

"Don't you dare trust any of these men that come around this house and don't get involved with them. If you do, everything I've worked so hard for will all be for nothing and I might as well give up."

"Don't worry about me. I have only one goal and that is to go to college if I can figure a way out to do that. Since now you told me this, how can I leave you with all that is going on? Surely you don't trust these men any more than you want me to trust them."

"I can take care of myself and I will. You are an entirely different story. They want you but I won't let them near you."

"I don't know about the other men that come around but don't you think that Bill drinks a lot?"

"He always did."

"Does he get rough with you?"

"He has never touched me, he kind of keeps to himself. I make dinner for him and put it in the oven. He knows it's where it is if he wants it. He even sleeps on the couch."

"So that's why the curtain is around the couch."

"For his privacy. That's the least I could do for him."

"But doesn't he throw things at you?"

"Oh, you mean the other night when he smashed dishes against the wall? He does that from time to time. Probably to let off steam but he doesn't mean anything by it. Just the alcohol he consumes."

"Do you ever ask him to stop the drinking?"

"First of all, it isn't any of my concern and it wouldn't do any good if I did. He'd still do it. Drinking probably helps him to forget everything he gets into."

"What should he need to forget?"

"Don't ask any more questions, Tabatha. You don't need to get into anything."

They busied themselves with dinner and setting the table for what it was. "I like how you always put a table cloth on this old wooden table, Mother."

"Yeah, it covers it up."

"Looks good that way."

"Never mind about that. You need to have your dinner and then disappear in your room before Bill comes home. I don't like any of the men around you."

"You don't trust them, do you?"

"No, I don't but I won't give them a chance."

"And then, that's the reason I come to see you at the Bar if you aren't home before me."

"That's it, exactly."

Tabatha wanted very much to ask Ann about going to the dance with Bruce but there just didn't seem to be an appropriate time. If she didn't want her to have anything to do with the men that came around the house, then she probably wouldn't like Bruce either. *I'm just going to have to tell Bruce the dance is out. I just can't do that.*

Chapter Thirty-One
The Outfield

The outfield had become a habit as the two of them continued to meet there every day. Getting together with Bruce encouraged Tabatha, yet, on the inside she feared everything would be over sooner than later. As always she'd have to flounder and make it on her own once again, just like before. Still, she didn't want to give up the meeting. Especially, since she had to figure out what her final escape plan would be and bouncing her thoughts off someone else made life feel easier. The deadline was coming closer every day. Even Ann wanted her to get out, on her own.

He is indeed my lifeline and that scares me. I'm not used to having someone around that appears to care for me. Then who is he?

They met. "Come, let me take you to that dance, Tabatha. Want to try and let me ask your mother today?"

"On the one hand I'd love nothing better but I really don't think she will even allow me to go with you."

"What brought you to that conclusion so suddenly?"

"I had a talk with her yesterday. I'll be surprised if she says yes."

"But your mother has never met me before. I'm sure I could make her like me."

"Oh you do? You really think that? I know I shouldn't but I'd like to see for myself if you can pull it off."

"Trust me. Remember, if it's okay with her, you can come to my place where I have friends that will put everything together for you. Believe me, this is as much for me as it is for you."

"But why me, Bruce? There are a lot of other girls that would love to go with you."

"I don't care about anyone else. You are the one I would like to see enjoy that dance and your graduation."

"Are you saying I'm a charity case?"

"No never, not on your life."

"You scare me. I'm too young for anyone to care."

"That's just not true, don't get me wrong. I don't plan on leading you astray. I wouldn't do that. Just be my friend and go to the dance with me. Make me happy."

"have an even better idea. Mom works at the bar. Come with me to see her there. We'll be on neutral ground, and I won't feel so bad."

"Let's go there then."

This was an easy plan for Tabatha. She could bring Bruce by and if she didn't approve it would only be a "sorry, no can do." The best part, her Mother would probably not feel threatened the same way she would in their home.

The local bar was only a few blocks away from the school. Tabatha had that uneasy feeling again. "You really want to charm my mother?"

"I'd love to do that. I'll bet she and I will get along really well."

They didn't say another word until they came closer to the entrance. "This is it, Bruce."

"I figured this would be the one."

"How could you know that?"

"How many Bars are there around here and then does your mother drive?"

"I don't know, but we don't have a car. So that's it, close enough to walk."

They entered the dimly lit bar trying to focus on their surroundings. Tabatha's eyes focused on Mark, the bar tender. He was leaning against the counter there ready to pour drinks.

"I'm going to have to *card* you kids. But Tabatha you aren't old enough for me to pour you a beer."

Bruce answered, "Just give us a couple of sodas."

"I'm just here to see my Mom. Is she around?"

"Let me get her."

Mark left.

"So this is where your Mother works? Hmm, some of my friends come in here from time to time."

Ann appeared, surprised to see Tabatha. "What are you doing here, Tabatha? Is school out already?"

"I really wanted you to meet Bruce. He came around to see if I could attend the graduation and the school dance with him."

"Hello Ma'am, I'm Bruce, one of the students from Melville High. As your daughter said, if I may, I'd like to take Tabatha to the school dance." Ann stood there listening without answering. "I want to take Tabatha because the school has chosen this time to present the scholarships and I'm certain your daughter will be awarded one. Now, I know what you are going to say, but my parents have friends with clothes that would fit your daughter to a tee. Normally, they would be discarded but I didn't think that was such a good idea and asked if Tabatha could wear any of them. With your permission, would you permit me to have the privilege of taking your daughter to this function?" Bruce was becoming a charmer. "This will be the last dance for her to attend at Melville High."

Ann was quiet for a few minutes. She continued to look Bruce over and then disappeared for a moment."

"Is this the cold shoulder I'm getting from her, Mark?"

"I don't think so. She wants to protect her daughter. Just let her think about it for a few minutes. I'll tell you what, if I have to, I'll tell her it's a good idea."

Soon she returned. "I don't know. When is it?"

"Actually, it is next Friday. Tabatha wouldn't let me ask you until today when she decided I could meet you at your work."

Ann looked at Bruce as if she was about to search him. "Haven't I seen you in here before?"

"Well, Ann, I don't know. Maybe we've met in the local grocery store. Somehow I find myself there more often then I care to admit. I go a lot of places, could be anywhere. Think maybe the local bank? I don't actually remember talking with you, though." It was true, he had never spoken to her but he had seen her and he had been in this very bar before.

Ann continued to busy herself around the bar, partly trying to ignore both Tabatha and Bruce.

Mark, seeing nothing was going to come of this visit, said, "Come on Ann give Tabatha a break. Bruce looks like he will take care of your daughter. She'll be fine with him. I'd be willing to wager over that." Mark wasn't saying anything, but he remembered quite well who Bruce was. He had recognized him coming in with a group of undercover police. He was acquainted with Sergeant Smith just slightly. He knew for certain this was law enforcement on an undercover assignment, but he wasn't about to blow Bruce's cover.

"Well, that might be okay but I don't know where I could get her anything in such short notice, let alone afford anything."

"Like I said, my family would be delighted to give clothes they don't need to Tabatha. She'll be the prettiest gal in the neighborhood. I'll have someone take pictures for you to have. Not only that, if you wanted to be present for the scholarship presentations, you are aware there is seating for family. I'm certain Tabatha would be delighted to have you come."

"I couldn't do that. I'm always working and don't like to fuss about myself. I wouldn't care for that scene. Since you brought it up, I'd love to have a picture of Tabatha in her outfit. Remember if you don't take care of my daughter, I'll have you arrested for something. Don't you dare do anything to her, you hear?"

"Of course. I take it that will be a yes?"

"Okay."

Chapter Thirty-Two
The Chicago Scene

———

"What do you think, Anita? Here we are in Chicago. We don't have any idea where we should start but we know your daughter should be here somewhere."

"I'm praying. Then when I find her, or if I find her, what will she think? Where have I been for her whole life?"

"Let's not go there just yet, Anita. We want to find her first."

"What if she's already in the drug scene?"

There the two of them sat dining at the Del Frisco contemplating their future encounters. They had just driven in and found a hotel but they were hungry. The atmosphere was pleasant and almost exciting. It was a new city, a new town and close to the lake.

"She should be turning sixteen in May, Tim and I don't even know my own daughter. Think about it, is she ready to graduate? How will she afford college? If she still is with George and Sam? Who would have reared her anyhow?"

"You're asking too many questions. We just got married and been on the move every day. We haven't even had time for a honeymoon. Let's just relax for a moment and finish our dinner first.

"I warned you Tim and that's why I wanted to go this on my own."

"I would never let you do that. By yourself, it wouldn't be possible."

They were quiet for during their dinner but Anita couldn't keep from thinking she needed to plan the next steps they would have to make.

"Didn't Officer Jim say something about notifying Sergeant Stumps?"

"He did. But how we find him will be more like finding a *needle in the haystack*. An impossible task."

"Not so fast, after we've finished our dinner we'll go to the police station and start the inquiry. Someone has to know him."

The two of them did just that. They made the inquiry at more than one place. "He must be on the North side."

"Do you have an address?"

"Sure, here, try this station." The officer handed him a paper with information of addresses they could search out.

They found the first station only to find that their officers are moved from time to time. After about five tries they found one station in the bad part of town.

"Why would you need to talk to Stumps?"

"We are looking for my daughter."

"A missing child?"

"She's been missing for sixteen years."

"And you are looking for her now?"

"It's a very long story. We almost caught up with them in Los Angeles when they disappeared into thin air. It's taken almost six years from there. Finally, we found out by chance that they might have come to Chicago. We just don't know where to look."

"We've scoured town after town, Anita and I."

"This part scares me the most."

"Why, Ma'am?"

"It's obvious to me that the area in your precinct is drug infested. I'm afraid."

"Afraid for yourselves? I could understand that."

Anita's hand shook. "No, sir, my daughter, I just don't know how I will find her."

"I'm officer Turner. I know Sergeant Stumps' major concentration is the drug scene. Trying to make a dent in making a difference. Maybe if I knew your daughter's name?"

"Her name is Tabatha, Sir."

"Is her sir-name the same as you?"

"No, I've since remarried to this man, Dr. Tim Conway. She would have been Tabatha Rosander."

"A Swedish name?"

"Yes, that's where I am from originally."

"Your husband?"

"Sir, I'm an American. I run a Shelter just north of Tijuana on the U.S. side, obviously near the Mexican border."

"You're here to find this young lady?"

"We both are, Sir."

"Let me go check on something. I won't be too long. Just make yourselves comfortable and I'll be back shortly."

Tim and Anita sat there and waited. "Here, Anita, instead of just sitting here, why don't you take a look at the *Chicago Times*."

"For more depressing news? Do you know that almost everything is about drugs around here? How many are dying due to violence? Do you realize Tim, my daughter, is in the middle of all that?"

"You are going to be a detriment to finding her if you don't calm down."

"Tell me, how do I do that?"

"We both know that God has to be in control. We can pray this through and somehow God has given me the comfort of His Spirit to know we are at least going in the correct direction."

"I need to hear that. I have to find Tabatha. A sixteen-year-old in this part of town scares me."

"So it should. To be of any help to her at all we have to be leveled minded."

"I know Tim. Help me."

"Ask God to do that for you."

"I have."

The wait seemed like an eternity when Officer Turner returned.

"Please, Officer, don't give us bad news. We've come a long way to find Tabatha."

"I'm going to take all your information down. Make a report and give it to Sergeant Smith. Let me check my calendar." He seemed to be thumbing through his schedule of notes. "Okay, I will make an appointment with him and tell him about the both of you and who you are looking for."

"When do we hear from you?"

"Where are you staying?"

"Put it this way. We just drove in this morning and don't have a clue where we should stay. Any suggestions?"

"Yeah, I definitely advise you not to stay anywhere around here. Here's a map of the city and I'll highlight a reputable Hotel you could stay at until I can get back to you."

Anita insisted, "Is our waiting for nothing, or is there a chance?"

"Until we hear differently, there is always hope. When you deal in this part of town, you can't just walk the streets and hope to find your daughter. That will never happen. We need to take all the information you've given us and put it together and maybe you can be of some help to us. I will let you know in a few days."

Tim and Anita left for the Hotel recommended to them. It was a good location but away from the drug dealers. They would be comfortable for the time.

This wasn't going to be an easy discovery for the police.

"Stumps, I need to meet with you as soon as I can."

"Turner? I haven't heard from you in years. What's up? Where are you anyhow?"

"Stumps, forget the small talk, I need to visit with you over a cup of coffee."

"Don't know Turner, I've been extremely busy. Working on a life and death case right now. It's really hard to get away from this kind of work. Sometimes, Turner, I wish I had your job as much as I like the investigation of my kind of work."

"This is extremely important to your case, Smith, I have to see you ASAP."

"Coming from you, I guess you really mean it."

"This time I do. It is absolutely imperative that we meet sooner than later."

Chapter Thirty-Three
Searching High Schools

"I don't know Tim. How long are we supposed to wait before we get a call from Officer Turner?"

"We need to trust he'll soon be in touch with us."

"It's too expensive for us to stay in this Hotel until he decides he's ready."

"We're okay with that, we can wait."

Anita wasn't to be kept away from trying to find Tabatha. They had to be very close to the right location or Officer Turner wouldn't have suggested the location. Or, maybe he wanted to keep them away from the very place Tabatha was being kept. There it was again. Anita couldn't help but feel she was in hiding with horrible men. Her Tabatha, she couldn't erase that thought.

"I have a novel idea, Tim."

"You have?"

"This is graduation time. Why not check to see what schools are in the precinct that Sergeant Smith is located."

"They wouldn't give us that information."

"So that means something is going on."

"We need to wait, Anita."

"You are asking me to wait when I think my daughter is in danger?"

Tim tried as hard as he could for he knew it was imperative that Anita be kept away from that scene. He had a gut feeling there was a case involvement they couldn't share just yet. He wouldn't dare mention that to Anita or she would indeed interfere and that could cause a worse outcome.

"Let me call Officer Turner. Maybe he can give me some kind of information."

"Please do that, Tim, please. I have to know."

Tim made the call to inquire if he could have the location where Sergeant Smith might be.

"I'm sorry, Dr. Turner. I can't actually give you that information."

"Why?"

"Okay, let me tell you this. He is involved in a very dangerous undercover operation. There are lives at stake and we don't want to interfere until the investigation has been completed."

"But that could be months."

"No, not at all, but it might be days. Just stay with me and we will be able to connect you to the Sergeant."

Anita wouldn't be quieted. She had to find her daughter and no one could stop her. She would look even if she had to do it alone. After all, it was her daughter who had been abducted.

"Why do you think Tabatha would be graduating already? Isn't sixteen too young?"

"Remember, she is my daughter. That's the best chance we have of finding her."

"Okay, whatever you think. How do we find the school?"

"There has to be a clue somewhere."

It was a clue they needed. There were numerous high schools scattered everywhere throughout the city, but which one would be the correct one? Anita grabbed the phone directory in the hotel room, thumbing through the yellow pages for high schools.

"Too many, Anita?"

"Yeah, where do I begin?"

"Just a few more days, and they'll have what they need, then we will get the call. There is no way Sergeant Smith could possibly stop to talk to us when he's in one of Chicago's major busts."

"You're talking about my daughter. I haven't been there for her on any of her sixteen years. She was stolen from my own arms."

"I know. There isn't any possible way they will disclose information to anyone that calls the school. To them you would be a total stranger."

"Oh, would I? I'm still carrying my green card with my maiden name on it. I can show them that she is my namesake."

"Remember, your namesake, is Bergin, your maiden name. You don't know if they're using Anton's or Ann's or even theirs. That's a hard one and Sergeant Smith will know."

Anita didn't want to hear that. She continued the search for possibly the right school. "But, which one? We'll actually have to go to each one. I have an idea, Tim. Let me look at the newspaper and see if I can find a schedule of graduations of the different schools."

"Okay, maybe we can busy ourselves looking while we wait for Officer Turner to call us and give us the word."

They found Newspapers all over town and made inquiries everywhere. Began asking people where the school locations in poverty stricken areas might be.

"The library, what about the library? Tim, they know everything about everything. We're in the 90s so with the computers they have there we should gleam some information."

"I'm only willing to ask where the schools are, not so much in going to the locations."

"Even if, they aren't having graduation ceremonies at least if I call each one that is in some of those locations, I can say I'm a relative of hers. They might tell me if she attends there."

Tim and Anita made their way to the local library to make inquiries. Names and phone numbers, Anita recorded all of them. "Here, Ma'am, but I don't think you should go to this one. Too many drug busts get reported in that neighborhood. I have about five that I know you don't want to get involved with."

Tim was interested. "Let me write that information down."

"Phone numbers, Tim, write the phone numbers down. Can you tell us if there is a published record of graduates for any of these schools?"

"There's a novel idea. Wouldn't have thought about that."

The librarian thought for a minute. "Who's Who Among American High Schools lists the names of some students. That doesn't always include deserving students. It's more for an advertising gimmick to see if proud parents or relatives will buy stuff from the advertising. It's been reported that factious names have been entered without verification. This is all according to information on the internet."

"We could look at the list."

"You are looking for a particular person?"

"I am, my daughter."

"You've lost touch with her?"

"I have. She was stolen from me as a baby. I've tracked her down to Chicago. Now I'm looking at schools."

"Have you gone to the police?"

"We're actually waiting on a phone call from Officer Turner with a precinct in a not so good part of town. He's asked us to wait until he can put us in touch with a Sergeant that works on the drug scene."

The Librarian wanted to be encouraging. "You should wait for him. This city can be very rough in certain parts and it really wouldn't be wise to go places you know nothing about."

"You don't understand, that is the very reason I want to find my daughter."

"How many years since you last saw her?"

"She turns sixteen at the end of May, so it's been that long."

The librarian insisted. "Please don't do this on your own. I don't want to read about another statistic. You really must wait on the Sergeant. They know what they are talking about. Please don't go. I'm sure you will find her if you wait but you might very well put her in jeopardy if you don't."

"Exactly what I've been saying, but what do you say to a Mother?"

Chapter Thirty-Four
Preparations

"Help! Help! This is an emergency, Smith. You said you could take care of this for me."

Bruce had the feeling he was being left in a jam. This had to come together but Sergeant Smith had said it could all be arranged, so it should be no sweat? At least that was where Bruce was coming from. A deal was a deal.

"What, Bruce? Take care of what? I don't even know what you are talking about. What was I supposed to take care of?"

"Clothes, Tabatha needs clothes for the dance."

"Oh, that, isn't that in a couple of weeks?"

"No, I need all that for tonight. The clothing that will fit Tabatha and it all has to be at my place this afternoon. I need someone who knows how to dress a young gal like her. She has to have the *works* but it has to be convincing that everything is *a hand-me-down,* in other words, no tags left on the clothing. My house has to look the part as well. If she should get suspicious we've lost everything and possibly Tabatha's life. Think about it."

"I'm thinking about it."

"Can you still pull it off?"

"Is there another way?"

"Sergeant, what are you saying?"

"We have to, right Bruce?"

"Remember, she will need everything from top to bottom. I need a hair dresser and a makeup artist as well."

"I detect panic from you."

"Please, that's not the word for it. Just tell me, who is going to help me?"

"How would I know? I don't know those kinds of things let alone people who do that stuff. You tell me, Bruce, whom should I get to help you?"

"Come on Smith, you said this wouldn't be a problem if I could get Tabatha to go to the prom." Bruce drew a deep sigh. "Please don't tell me you are going to bail on me, are you?"

"Give me a couple of weeks and see what I can come up with."

"Smith, I don't have a couple of weeks. The prom is tonight. I have to have the stuff now."

"I'll have to talk to some of my connections. What day next week do we have to get this together?"

"Smith, I told you, it is tonight. I have to have this done for this evening!"

"When are you picking her up?"

"I'll have her at my place at 3 o'clock."

"That soon? I just don't know."

"Come on Smith. I need you to be there for Tabatha or the whole case is in jeopardy. You know that and you said it would be no problem to get this stuff put together."

"Nancy could be your girl. She's the smartest gal I know and she owes me one."

"It's not just smarts this time, Smith. It has to be about style. I need someone who not can make Tabatha into a Princess."

"A princess? That's a very tall order. We'll try our best."

"Don't say that. It's my life. It's actually, not my life, but Tabatha's life."

"Okay, okay. Nancy will be at your place before you get back with Tabatha. I promise."

"You better."

It was settled, Tabatha would get to meet Nancy, the gal who could perform miracles and the best in the business. That is, she was a furniture designer but was she as clever with clothing and makeup? True she was a very good-looking stylish gal. Who knew she could pull this off? Yet, she was Sergeant's gal.

I knew it. I should have hired a specialist to do this. It's too late for that. I've already buttonholed Sergeant into making it his obligation. Time would tell very quickly if he had made the right decision.

"Oh God, I'm in trouble! Please help me!"

Now Bruce was running. He had to arrange his house so that it would look as if he lived with his parents. *I left the dishes in my sink just like a bachelor would. She'll know I'm living alone.* Bruce grabbed his phone. *My house keeper doesn't come until Monday and that's definitely too late.*

I need a phone number. He found a name he hoped he could call.

The phone rang, once, twice. *Lord, I need this person not tomorrow but now.* Someone answered. "Please, Doris, I really need your help right now."

"Oh, Bruce, how good to have you call. How can I help? By the way Jimmy and I have a dinner date tonight. Remember that new restaurant near the new Mall?"

"Don't tell me that, Doris, I need to have you come and straighten up my house before three this afternoon."

"What?"

"Before you say no, let me tell you just about as much as I can. I'm involved in a sensitive case." Bruce divulged as little of the situation as he could. "Please, I know if I try I won't get my place in order on time and then it blows up in my face and that's not the half of it."

"Stop it Bruce, I'll be over in five. I'll do just as much as I can and if you don't mind, I'll have to change at your place and have Jimmy pick me up there."

"Perfect. Even if I bring Tabatha back before you leave, I may have to introduce you as someone you aren't."

"Remember, I'm too young to be your parent."

"Put some heavy makeup on or give me another excuse."

"Just go get her, you don't have that much time." Doris put down the receiver at the other end of the call but Bruce, with telephone still in hand was frozen. What was the plan?

I can't remember telling Tabatha where I would pick her up and when. Would we meet in the outfield on an occasion such as this? Shouldn't I pick her up at home? But I have never been allowed there. The Bar? Would she want me to do that?

Must be we were meeting in the outfield. Oh, God, please have her be there."

Bruce was gone to find Tabatha.

Chapter Thirty-Five
Where Is Tabatha

"Tabatha, wasn't this the day for Bruce to take you to the Prom?"
"I think so."
"He's not here yet?"
"No, and I'm beginning to think something went wrong."
"I don't want you in this house when the men get here. You have to go or lock yourself into your room and don't come down. But be sure it is locked and don't make a sound."
"That's okay, I'll be gone."
"Where are you going by yourself?"
"I'll go over to the Church. Somebody must be there. I'll make sure not to come back until there are no cars parked out front."
"Then go. I hear cars pulling up, go."
Tabatha left out the side door. She didn't have a choice. How Bruce would ever find her she didn't know. *I don't know what to do. Like I told Mom, I'll walk over to the church. If Pastor Nelson is in his study, maybe I can pass the evening talking with him. He might have some words of encouragement.*

"Where's Tabatha, Ann? We came to pick her up."
"She's not here. She's gone."
"You better tell us because we're going after her."
"You can't and I don't intend telling you where she went."

Sam turned to George. "She'll be at her graduation at Melville High. I wouldn't go there if I was you, too many people there. Wait until tomorrow."

"Let's go Sam. We'll get her there. It'll be easy."

It didn't take her long to get to the church but to her dismay, no one but the gardener was around. *Well, at least there is a person. I just don't want to be alone right now.*

"I'm surprised, Tabatha, what are you doing here? Isn't your Prom tonight?"

"Yeah."

"Aren't you supposed to go to that? Don't you have a date?"

"I thought I did but we never got to discuss where we were to meet. So here I am."

"I can't leave you here alone, why don't I take you home?"

"Can't do that. My Mom has company that I didn't want to get involved with, so I can't do that. Please don't worry about me, I'll be okay. I'm sure I can go home in about an hour. Those guys should be gone by then and Mom will want me by then."

"Don't like just leaving you but it is still daylight. That's the nice thing about summer months."

The gardener left and there Tabatha was, alone. Not at all what she wanted. Especially, now after her mother had asked her not to stay home. That just couldn't be good.

Bruce just knew he could find Tabatha in the *Outfield*. It had always been their meeting place. He knew how much she didn't want him at her house so she must be there. He quickly drove his car there and as he scoured the field, he saw no one. *Of course, no one would be here. Everyone was getting ready for the Prom. What do I do now?* Bruce continued walking around the school. She just had to be somewhere around the building. Yet, not a soul, no one was anywhere near the school and not even on the grounds.

Maybe I should check her house. He drove to Tabatha's home when he saw the two men get out of their vehicle. *I should arrest those guys right now. Be done with the whole situation. I can't do that. I would blow the whole case wide open. They'd get free and I could kiss my investigating job goodbye. If I can't pull this off, life won't be worth anything. I'm here to protect that gal.*

He wasn't really sure of that anymore. He was afraid Tabatha was only his date because he really cared for her. After seeing the drug dealers at her house, he knew he wanted to come in with Machine guns and blast them out of her life forever. *I can't do that, Lord, can I? Then show me where she is.*

Bruce sat on the front stairs of the school. *Where else have I been with Tabatha? That's right, we were in church together.* Bruce sped off to the church. *I don't see her but if she isn't here, where can I go?* He began walking around the building, hesitating at the back stairs. *There she is. I found her.*

"Tabatha, I am so sorry we never made the arrangements for where to meet."

"Not half as sorry as I was. Didn't know what to do. My Mother didn't want me at home so I had to go somewhere. I was hoping Pastor Nelson would have been here. He always has a very level head and knows what to say. I don't mind telling you, I was scared."

"Now I really am sorry, Tabatha." Bruce knew he needed to change the view, talk about the Prom and how wonderful it would be. "Okay, we have the biggest surprise of your life waiting for you. You will be the most beautiful girl at Melville High."

"I will be? I would prefer to be inconspicuous. That would be my choice."

"Please humor me, Tabatha, you are my date and I want to brag you up."

"What if I don't meet your standards?"

"You've already exceeded everything just by being you."

"You're making me feel self-conscious."

"Sorry, but you will be surprised."

◆ ◆ ◆ ◆

Tim and Anita were busy now. They only had a few schools left to call. "Look, a list. Could it be?"

"Okay, let me read it." Both of them were glued to the local papers. "They don't say who's who or what they might be awarded but that's the list."

"We need to find that school."

"I think, Anita, we have to call Officer Turner."

"He'll just put us off and make us wait. I have to see her now."

"We're calling Officer Turner, no matter the decision we make for ourselves. They need to know what our thinking is just in case there is more to the story than just us trying to find Tabatha. We can't just grab her and run."

"Oh, I'd never do that. She has to be able to make some of her own decisions. She has to want to meet me. I just wanted to see her at the graduation. Have the privilege of being there for her whether she knows me or not."

Tim called Officer Turner. "What? You will be here in a few minutes?" Tim quickly put the receiver back in its cradle.

"What was that about?"

───────────────

"Stumps, we have a problem."

Officer Turner explained the details. "Ouch, Stumps, not so loud, I can hear you, I'm not deaf."

"Then you know what to do."

"How do you expect me to do that? They haven't committed a crime."

"Like I said, you know what to do, just do it."

Chapter Thirty-Six
The Party

    This was going to be a tough time for Tabatha. On the one hand she had allowed herself the pleasure of the handsomest man at Melville High to bring her to the prom. She didn't know how she dared allow this to happen. Her heart could just as easily give her away and she didn't even know if this guy, Bruce was even for real. She knew the next step would be a broken heart and in her circumstances, could she even deal with that possibility? He was just a caring guy and Tabatha knew she came from the wrong *side of the tracks.* She had no heritage to offer let alone a right to a life like his. Didn't he know who she was? That was precisely the problem, she had no idea. The lady that had reared her, was she really her mother? When she thought about it, her name wasn't even the same. So what was up with that? Could she ask why? Asking would give an answer she might not be able to deal with. Going with the flow, always had been her best bet.

    "Tabatha, you look lovely."

    "Thank you, Marybeth. Who did you come with?"

    "Jerry, you know him, from Math class?"

    "Okay, I think I do. The school isn't exactly that small but hey, I recognize him. So how is it going for you?"

    "Wonderful, I thought the two of you were going to be busy tonight."

Bruce "I convinced Tabatha that everything we had to do could wait on such an event as this. So here we are to enjoy it with everyone else."

Suddenly, Bruce's phone started ringing. "I thought everyone knew I would be busy tonight. Let me get this." He hesitated, "Smith?"

"You have to hide Tabatha somewhere, and keep her out of sight."

"We are in the middle of activities and the awards are going to come up soon."

"Bruce, listen to me, you have to get her out of there immediately. Tell you later."

That was it. Smith had given him orders and he would have to fulfill them to keep her safe. Something was going down. Now the dilemma was to pull Tabatha out of all the activities he had worked so hard for her to experience. He had to pull her away for her own security.

Marybeth was still talking to Tabatha. "In a couple of hours they want to do the *catwalk* so we can show off our gowns. You're a winner, you know."

"I'm going to pass on that. I wouldn't even know how to walk."

"It's not that hard. Just watch the others and do the same."

Bruce interrupted. "Please excuse us, Marybeth, Tabatha and I have to get on to some unfinished business. We'll try to be back in just a bit. Come with me Tabatha."

"What happened? It sounded as if a guy named Smith called you? What's up with that?"

"I heard you say you really didn't want to go on display, right?"

"I did say that and really, I'd love to do whatever it is to get out of all that nonsense."

"Come, let's go."

Bruce whisked her out of the building and into his car. "Bruce, what are you going to do with me?"

"Nothing, I promise. We can sit in my car and just wait."

"Wait for what?"

"We'll go back in shortly."

Tabatha was afraid, but she wasn't sure of what.

"Tim, I so hope we find Tabatha."

"We should have waited for Officer Turner. We don't know what we are getting ourselves into."

"They'll keep putting us off and I have to see her."

"Let's call a cab, then we will actually get to where we are going. I'm not at all familiar with the area and I kind of think we'll be safer that way."

It wasn't long before they drove up to the Melville High. People were milling about in and out of the auditorium. "If you introduce yourself as Doctor, maybe they'll let us in."

"All we can do is try."

It didn't take Officer Turner more than ten minutes when he arrived at Tim and Anita's hotel. The hotel attendant made the call to their room. "Sorry, Sir, there is no answer. They aren't answering the phone."

Turner flashed his badge. "What's the room number?"

"Are they in trouble with the law?"

"Room number, please."

"212, second floor at the top of the stairs. Before you go up, they left in a Cab and said they were going to a graduation ceremony so I called the Cab for them. I believe they said something like Melville High? Would that be a place you are interested in?"

"When did they leave?"

"It hasn't been five minutes."

Officer Turner put his car in full speed to catch up to the cab.

Then the announcement came from the Superintendent of Schools. "Now we will start on Scholarships. The first is a complete four-year Scholarship of your choice ... Tabatha Rosander.

Everyone waited in suspense. There was no Tabatha. She had disappeared. The hall fell in silence, waiting for Tabatha.

Marybeth told her date, Jerry, "I just talked to her. She was here a minute ago."

Someone was asking, "Where is Tabatha, has anyone seen her?" The students looked surprised, someone said, "I just saw her, she was here a minute ago."

Tim and Anita were stopped at the entrance to the auditorium.

"Sorry, folks, I know what you told me, but I can't let anyone in."

"Why? There's a student in there that is my daughter."

By now Officer Turner came up behind them. "You two really do need to come with me."

"We haven't done anything. You can't arrest us."

"Just come with me."

Soon people started exiting the auditorium talking to one another, "I wonder where Tabatha disappeared to. Wasn't she with Bruce? I thought he was a really nice boy."

Anita and Tim heard that. "Did you people say Tabatha?"

"We did. Do you know where she disappeared to?"

"No, but we'd sure like to know."

"We were surprised. She was just awarded a four-year scholarship for the College of her choice. She does deserve it, believe me. I saw her a few minutes ago but I don't know where she went. They'll find her."

"Who was she with, do you know?"

Marybeth said, "Yeah, the handsomest guy at Melville High."

Tim nudged Anita. "Don't say it. Nobody knows us here. We need to do what Officer Turner is asking us to do."

"It's for your safety." Officer knew he had to get them out of the area.

"Officer, I don't care about my safety, I just have to know that Tabatha is safe."

"Please, come with me, it will work out well if you follow my instructions."

It was the hardest think that Anita had to do. A daughter she hadn't seen for sixteen years, since her birth was at her finger tips and now she was told, not yet. She couldn't see her now. She would have to wait. What kind of trouble was she in?

"I have to inform you both, that I am going to have to put you on house arrest at the hotel. You will not be able to leave until you get the okay from us."

"Tim, can they do that to us?"

"They have good reason, I'm sure." Tim turned to Officer Turner, "Please assure us that this is Anita's Tabatha and that she will be kept safe."

"We are doing our very best."

"I'm glad, Bruce, that you rescued me from all the public display scene."

"It would have been fun to see you up there with everyone else. Believe me, that wasn't my fault."

"Where are we going now?"

"Just let's sit in the car for a couple of minutes."

"Tell me, who is this Stumps and why did we leave early?"

"Don't worry about that, but take a look over there."

"Cops? What's going on?"

"Don't know."

"George, if you hired me to be your bodyguard, you better *back up the truck.* The place is surrounded by Cops."

"I see that."

They stood in the parking lot watching intently. "What does that mean, George? We're going to have to get out of here."

"I'm going to get what I came for. I haven't spent all these years and paid all this money on rearing a child to find I have lost her?"

"Don't think I can be your bodyguard if you're getting into kidnapping. I'm not going there."

"You'll do as your told or it'll be up for you. Do you get that?"

"You think you can get away with that?"

"Don't try me."

"I'll get what I want, if not today, tomorrow."

Soon, everything began to subside as the people streamed out of the auditorium. It almost looked like an emergency evacuation. Bruce got out of the car to inquire from some of the students leaving.

"What happened in there?"

"Don't know why, but after the scholarships where announced, the cops showed up and next thing we knew we were being escorted out."

"Tell me, do you remember who got the scholarships."

"Tabatha, of course, we all knew she would."

Tabatha jumped out of the car. "What? You mean me?"

"Oh there you are. What happened that you disappeared?"

Bruce spoke up. "I got a call and was told that something was going on and I didn't want us to be a part of that. I grabbed Tabatha and left. I know we just have to report to the office on Monday and Tabatha will be able to pick up her scholarship."

"I always thought you were somehow connected. At least law enforcement is on top of all this. Kept us safe yet again."

"They try."

"Like I said before, what do I do with all these clothes?"

"You want me to hold on to all of that for you?"

"I do. I don't know where to keep it at my house and I don't want to explain it to anyone until I am ready."

"I can do that."

"Do you know what that means?"

"What?" asked Bruce?

"I have a place to go after school lets out. I can maybe stay at home until I leave for College. Do you suppose, *soul-mate*, you could help me figure that out, if you don't mind?"

"I'd be delighted to. I can arrange for you to stay at Nancy's place tonight if you'd rather not go home?"

"I don't think so. Mom will wonder where I am and worry that something went wrong especially if she finds out the cops were all around the school. Thanks for everything anyhow. I know my debt to you can never be repaid as I would wish but someday, maybe I can."

"Meet on the outfield?"

"Perfect."

Tabatha was still in disbelief, "Me, a scholarship?"

"Come on, Tabatha. You worked very hard for that."

"Yeah, only because what else could I do? That was all there ever was for me."

"It paid off, don't knock it and I still say you earned it."

The house was quiet but Bruce watched while Tabatha walked through and closed her front door. Little did Bruce know what the future was about to serve.

Chapter Thirty-Seven
Tuesday Morning

It was early Tuesday morning as Tabatha rubbed her eyes. The day after the graduation ceremonies, no wonder she couldn't wake up. *I've got to get moving if I'm going to get to school on time.* Brushing her teeth, she began to think, *I still don't know what all that ruckus was about last night. Oh, well, they say I have a Scholarship and for that I'm very thankful. Hopefully, the rest of my life will work out. I'll be out of this house and on my own.*

Everything seemed a little strange. *I'm so glad Bruce allowed me to leave my clothes and stuff with him. That reminds me, I'm going to have to pick up my graduation papers when I get to school.* Tabatha wasn't sure if the odd feeling was about last night or something else. *It was quiet overnight, and usually Bill comes in drunk. Didn't hear him.*

"Hi Mom, I'll just grab this breakfast bar, bottle of water and be off or I'll be late. But Mom, where is Bill? I didn't hear him come home last night. Usually, I hear him quite loudly but I slept right through everything."

"Forget him, how did it all go last night?"

"I got a four-year scholarship."

"Wonderful."

"We didn't even get through the evening when the cops stormed the auditorium."

"What happened? Did you get involved?"

"No, Bruce pulled me out. Somehow he had a phone call and the next thing I knew we were gone."

Ann gave a sigh of relief. "I'm glad you were with Bruce. At least he kept you safe."

I have to go pick up my papers and we still have a few more classes to get through. Why, I don't know."

"Don't worry, it's always done that way."

"But what about Bill? What happened to him?"

"Don't you worry about him. Bill had to go away for a while. He'll be back, as he always is."

"I don't get it. You know where he is?"

"He'll be back, soon."

"How soon? And if you know, where is he?"

"Just go to school. I'm busy and I don't need to be questioned by you. Don't be getting smart with me."

Something was strange. Why would Mom act defensive about Bill's whereabouts? As far as I know Mom doesn't even care for him. He doesn't much matter to her, he is only here for George and Sam.

Tabatha wasn't hardly on the school grounds when Marybeth met up with her. "Hey, Tabatha, where is your Dad?"

"I think he is away on business. Why?"

"I can't believe you don't know. My aunt told me to keep quiet, but he's in jail. I figured you should know that already."

"I don't even know that. Mom didn't tell me that."

"Sorry, like I said, I'm not supposed to say anything. See you later."

That kid, why doesn't she just go away? Just because her Aunt is the school principal she thinks she can get away with being a gossip. I hate her! What a horrible day this is turning out to be. I wish Bruce would have been here right about now. I needed him.

Tabatha felt the walk to school a bit far because she wasn't feeling too well either. Every muscle in her body ached. *I'll get over it like I do everything else. Just get over it--I need to get over it. But I am very hot and this is a cold spring day.*

One of her teachers noticed, "Tabatha, you look as though you don't feel well. You have a fever, go see the school nurse."

Tabatha complied as the nurse wrote a note for her parents to keep her home the rest of the week until she would be better.

"Why didn't you tell your parents you weren't well?" Nurse Jane always seemed to care.

"Don't know. I thought I might be okay later in the day. But, if I feel well enough, I'll be back tomorrow."

"You don't need to push yourself, the principal says you can finish up when you get better."

"Thank you but I will only stay home if I need to. If I'm better tomorrow, I'll be here."

Tabatha walked the short distance to her home, being ill didn't make the distance any easier. When she approached her home, she noticed extra cars on the property. *I'd better try the back entrance first and then if all appears well, I'll walk in and give my greetings. It would be better not to walk into my house without knowing. Okay, so Bill is gone but what about Mom? If there is a feud going on, I don't want to be around.* That was all too common for Tabatha's comfort. With a machine shop directly on one side of the house and an alley way running along the back but adjacent to the alley was a lumberyard. Virtually no neighbors to report any unusual behaviors. She knew she needed to be careful here. *I don't want to get into it with those people.*

Walking through the overgrown weeds, Tabatha approached the house. With walls without insulation and because the men were in a shouting match, it seemed, she could overhear the conversations. She stopped dead in her tracks, hiding behind the porch pole next to the steps hidden in the tall grass. Peering over to see through the window, she saw one, maybe two men? They were loud and certain of what they were demanding. "You need to give us the money if you think you want to keep her!"

"What have you done to Bill? Where is he?"

"He never was any good," *that must be George, he has the scar.* "We got caught on a robbery last night. He was our excuse because he was about to go soft on us. We couldn't afford that."

"Let me get this right, you robbed the bank and hung the blame on him?"

"George had that planned. He had Bill in the get-a-way car with the sock over his face. We left out the back and the cops spotted the car and grabbed him. It's an easy scape-goat, George."

"Knock it off, Sam, or I'll frame you next."

"That wasn't very smart, George. He was your bookkeeper. That's why we are here, Ann. We need the money he has on the books."

"Don't look at me. Bill and I never shared your business practices. It isn't something I'd get involved in."

"You are going to find his stuff and give it to us."

"Sorry, I know nothing. Go visit him in jail and let him tell you where everything is."

"George can't do that. He has to look clean."

"That has nothing to do with me. I'm only here to take care of Tabatha. That's the beginning and end of my story."

"That wasn't too smart. He was the money handler, George."

"I am very aware of that Sam, but I needed a *fall guy*, so it was either you or him, Sam."

"So now you want us to get into kidnapping?"

"Does that surprise you?" as Ann's comment.

"It wasn't kidnapping when we gave Tabatha to you Ann. That was a rescue."

"George, you call that a rescue of mercy?"

Sam knew very well what that was all about.

"We need the money now. Bill isn't here to hand it over so Ann, we're telling you to give it to us."

"Sorry, I already told you I have nothing. Bill never told me anything about *the business* and I never paid any attention. All I do is go to work every day and with my paycheck take care of Tabatha and myself. Bill takes care of himself."

"Bill always gave us cash for the stash. So where is it?"

"Stop it. I told you what I know. Bill doesn't tell me and I don't ask. I make it my business to stay out of that stuff."

George insisted, "You are going to have to take Bill's place whether you like it or not. We gave him a box to stash now we want the money."

"You should've thought about that before you let him go into the slammer. Go ask him."

"You have to know where Bill kept it or if you can't pay, you know the alternative."

"But I don't have any money!" Ann was horrified.

"We almost had Tabatha at the graduation ceremonies but the cops came from nowhere."

Tabatha was in total shock. *Take me to where? Why are they talking about me?* By this time, she had sunk low in the grass where she was sure she couldn't be seen.

"No! You can't have her. You gave her to me when she was a baby and I've taken care of her all these years. I intend to keep her safe."

"Then pay up. And furthermore, we want it now!"

"Where can I get money? There isn't any more. You locked up your pool of money, remember?"

"We don't exactly believe you. By now you should have a stash hidden in this house somewhere."

"I don't. As far as I know everything Bill had he gambled away and drank the rest. He might have kept back enough for you but you'll have to ask him for that."

"Well, guess what, it's your problem now. You come up with the money. We will be back and you better have it!"

"By the way, we were at the school last night to pick up Tabatha, but somebody got wind of something going down, so the cops had the auditorium surrounded. Know that we will be back and you will have to have found the money or we come for her."

The fever wasn't so important now as Tabatha walked away from the house. She walked around the block at least five times. *Who am I, anyhow? Mom just said those guys gave me to her. Where do they want to be taking me? Now know. I don't belong to this family. I was right all along. This is all too weird, maybe I'll just wake up in a minute and that is wishful thinking. This for real.* There was no room for tears as shock set in.

Going to the police was almost not an option. In the first place, the police would believe she was a *run-a-way* and bring her back to discuss the situation with Ann and her so called father who was now absent. Would Ann hand her over to these men in an effort to save herself? If she could prove she wasn't Ann's daughter after all it would mean foster care. In the end, these men wanted her and would claim her anyhow. There was no winning this time. Either way, she would be sold to the highest bidder.

Chapter Thirty-Eight
Running

    After walking as far as she could think to go, Tabatha turned back toward the house. It appeared quiet now so she crept up the stairs into her room crying herself to sleep.

    Morning came, Tabatha still didn't feel her best but she could feel the anger fill her soul. It would have to be God helping her now. She would slip out the side door before her Mother would awaken. Being well or not, she couldn't stay home. It was hard for her to get her mind around these men wanting to sell her like an animal. She knew she could not roam the streets nor could she get a job at 16 years of age. Should she lie about her age? Would someone hire her? How could she go back now? Where would she stay?

    It was too early for classes as Tabatha found herself back on the outfield sitting on the grass with her head in her hands. More thoughts began coming. Maybe she could figure this out. She knew she couldn't tell her mother she had overheard the conversation. She knew she needed time to find out who she was. Maybe the Red Cross? How would they know how to search for information she didn't even have? *If only I knew who I really am.*

    While Tabatha was still in deep thought, Bruce arrived, not trying to frighten her as he stood there. Startled for a moment Tabatha blurted out, "Bruce, where did you come from? I didn't see you."

    "I know. When you didn't show after school yesterday, I asked the principal. She said you were sent home due to illness."

    "I don't mean to be changing the subject, but I could use your help."

    "Tell me how."

"Remember, I told you I didn't think I belonged to my family? Well, I don't."

"How did you find that out for sure?"

Tabatha told Bruce the conversation she had overheard. "What do I do? Where do I go? The Red Cross is always locating people. Do you suppose that would work?"

Bruce was elated. This was one more piece of the puzzle he desperately needed. Not because of Tabatha's dilemma but because now he could begin the rescue work.

"If you heard that, how is your Mother going to come up with money for these guys?"

"I was thinking ..."

"I have a better idea. Come home with me and we'll do some brain storming. That might be quicker. I don't think time is on your side."

"Could we do that now? Mother doesn't even know that I'm ill yet; I'll give her the teacher's note later and then I can get started on the research."

"Let's give it a shot."

They were back at Bruce's house where all the preparations to the Prom had happened. Tabatha remembered the house just as it was. To her, it was all so neat and in order on the outside as it was on the inside. Bruce's maid had already been there for the week to make it sparkle. Once again, Bruce opened the double doors that led them into the living room.

"Here, Tabatha, I have a study to the left. Let's sit in here and maybe brainstorm on what to do next."

"You still have my stuff from the dance?"

"I do. I put your clothes in the spare bedroom you used to get ready for the dance. Oh, and I picked up your scholarship, it's in this envelope in this file. Do you want to see it?"

"Not now. I may never be able to make use of that."

"You will if I can help it. I'm keeping everything of yours safe. I don't want to lose anything. It's here in my desk so anytime you think you want any of these things, just give the word."

"I keep thinking, I really like your house but don't tell me your parents are still away?"

"This house is just a home. It allows me to get done what I need to."

"Where are your parents?" Tabatha wouldn't let it go.

Bruce's couldn't tell her he was on special assignment for her sake. She couldn't know that but so far she was in the game with him. He had to find her background. He had to know so that he could help her survive.

"They're still away on business. "

"Convenient, huh?"

"No, that's what they do."

"What kind of work?"

"My Dad is with the FBI." This was the total truth.

"Is that what you intend to do with your life?"

"Thought about it."

"Good, help me investigate my life, Bruce. I need all the help I can get."

"Tell me everything you know about yourself. Where you first remember and all that happened along the way. Maybe then we can fit the pieces together." This was what Bruce needed. Now he could get the rest of the story they needed to help Tabatha find out her beginnings.

"Let me think. We moved from Los Angeles to Chicago. I remember that because I didn't want to go. George said if I would keep sassing him he would lock me up."

"Did he ever lock you up?"

"My mother or as I now know, Ann wouldn't have any part of it. She told me to never trust anyone that came to the house. I'd either have to go to the library or the bar and do my studies. I've always had to report to her. The other place I was allowed to be on my own was the church."

"We moved to Chicago when I turned 10. Mom wanted to bake a birthday cake for me when George and Sam turned up to move us to Chicago. When we finally got to Chicago we met up with Bill, my so-called make-believe Father. We moved again to where we are now when I started school in my sophomore year. I remember my mother saying it was for George's sake that we were to appear to be a normal family. I could never understand that should keep the cops away. None of those guys are related to me. I keep thinking I'd like to search for my name in the records. It has to come up somewhere."

"Now that's a good idea, If they aren't going on an alias, that would work. The other plan is to check out what was going on around the year you were born. Something had to go down about that time."

"Here's a thought, if Bill is in jail right now, couldn't you ask him?"

"Maybe with my Dad in Law Enforcement, I might have connections that could help us find information. Why don't you let me find the information about Bill? With the name difference, it's likely that what you heard does really mean none of these people should have had anything to do with you."

"I guess you are right. George and Sam said as much."

"But we probably have to call it a day. I'll take you home but you have to make a few promises. If all doesn't go well tonight for you, meet me in the outfield. That has to be our meeting place. Somehow you have to call me. Here, take this."

"What's that?"

"A cell phone, let me show you." Bruce went through a quick scenario to show her how to call him.

"This is cool. I promise I'll use it only if I have to."

"Remember to call me Tabatha, it doesn't matter what time of day or night."

Chapter Thirty-Nine
At the House

It seemed that Tabatha was safe for the moment, no unusual commotions around the house. All was quiet, no one in the house but Ann sitting on the sofa with her eyes glued to the barely audible TV. Her gaze terrified Tabatha. It was obvious that Ann didn't have any idea on what to do next. These circumstances had to be beyond anything she had to face up to this point.

Tabatha pulled off her shoes slipping up the staircase, locking the door behind her. It was a hard and sleepless night as she pondered how she would face these men if they returned to take her hostage.

The next morning, they were having breakfast together when Ann remembered, "The school called yesterday to tell me you were ill and that they sent you home with a note. Where's the note? You haven't given it to me. Why didn't you come home? Where were you? She said you were to stay in for the rest of the week."

"I thought you were too busy yesterday. I saw a lot of people around the house from down the street and decided maybe I shouldn't be around so I went for a long walk." *I hope she buys that story.*

Ann look relieved.

Good, she thinks I'm not aware of anything.

However, Ann hadn't forgotten the note. "Where's the note the school gave you, Tabatha?"

"I must have lost it. I wasn't feeling very well when I was walking and it was late when everything settled."

"Don't you think you should come with me and rest in one of the back rooms at the bar? You know I don't want you can't be here without me."

"I'll be fine and I'm much better today. We just have to wrap up stuff at school and I can do my college inquiries today. It will be easier for me that way."

Ann didn't question anything.

Instead of school, Bruce and Tabatha were hot on the investigating trail as they pursued every possible avenue with nothing but dead ends to show for their work. Tabatha couldn't know that she had been under investigation since Bruce stepped into the picture and as a result both he and Tabatha had to pursue possibilities to see if they could find information somewhere. Even the Red Cross inquiry came back with nothing.

"I'm beginning to think you are from some another planet."

"How I wish, that would make everything easier. I could disappear and this would be over with."

"Not sure I would like that. You've become too much a part of my life already."

"Maybe I'm just a figment of your imagination?"

"I've made you into a real person because I care?"

"Oh, so you do care about me?"

"Of course I care."

"Bruce, there has to be something."

"You've seen all that I've seen but I have an idea. I know someone who could help us, would you mind if we met together? My friend could give us the information on Bill as well."

"Bruce, if I do that, they'll want me to go into Foster care or with my luck, they would send me home because they'd think I am a *run-a-way.*"

"Actually, I can promise that won't happen. Maybe if you give me permission, I'll talk to my friend first and see where it gets us."

"I'm afraid."

"I know you are but we have to find you somewhere."

"Before we do any of what you suggest, I think I have to go home while Mother is at work. I'm going to snoop in her bedroom. She must have my documents somewhere in the house. We've lived there six years already and I am registered at Melville. She must have had something around about me. I already know George and Sam want money from Ann. The next visit will have them turning the house upside down but I have to do that before they do."

"Let me come and be the look out."

"I don't want you to do that. I can't let you get involved."

"Come on, Tabatha, I'm already involved! Remember, you're my *Soul-mate* and I'm standing here offering to be the look out!"

"Well, okay, but you have to be invisible. If someone shows, you disappear! If they have any idea about what's going on, I'm *dead meat* but you don't have to be."

"I'll play the invisible man, I promise. Do you still have your phone?"

"You mean your phone? Yes, I have it."

"If you get stuck, you need to call."

"I promise."

"You wait out here."

"I can follow you in. I can hide if they come while we are still in there."

"Hide in that house? Are you kidding me, there is no place to hide. Stay outside, I'll be back before you know it."

Bruce could do nothing but watch from his car while Tabatha entering the house. He knew anything could go wrong. *Why don't I just tell her I'm a police officer and demand to go with her... but then I risk her running?*

Chapter Forty
The Coast is Clear

Tabatha looked in every direction. Gingerly she crept toward the side door. The quietness was deafening to her ears, though it was what she needed. Every spider that hung on the outside wall was startling. It appeared the coast was clear and the house seemed empty. *If I can hear people talking from my upstairs bedroom, surely I could hear if someone was in this house.* Ann's bedroom door was slightly ajar so Tabatha nudged it. Another confirmation there was no one around. *Where would she keep information about me?* Tabatha carefully opened every drawer she could find. *Something has to be here somewhere. I'm so scared.*

For comfort, Tabatha hesitated, should she call Bruce? Why not? She punched the necessary buttons. Bruce answered, "I'm coming!"

"No, please, if I need you, I can just redial, but I've looked everywhere in every drawer and can't find anything."

"Is there a desk or a file cabinet?"

"No, I don't see anything."

"Closet, look in the closet."

"Oh, I remember. A secret room that Bill said was out of bounds. It's unlocked, let me look. Okay, there's a safe in there and I wouldn't know where to look for the combination."

"I'm coming." Bruce closed the phone. He had watched where Tabatha had entered and did the same. He carefully entered the kitchen and saw another room. *Tabatha must be in there.* He whispered, "It's me. Show me the safe."

"Where would anyone keep the combination?"

"No time for that, Tabatha, let me try." Bruce pulled from his pocked a tiny plunger that he attached to the safe putting the other end to his ear.

"What are you, a safe cracker? Do you always carry that thing with you wherever you go?"

Bruce wasn't about to disclose his identity. "I need total silence to hear this." It took all of a minute as he turned the dial first in one direction and then in the other. Back again to hear the final click. "We've got it!"

Tabatha thumbed through the inside drawers of the safe. "Look, Bruce, a file with my name?"

"Take it. What's this? Money and a lot of it, stash it in your purse."

Bruce turned to look in the dark corner of the room. "Let's look there."

Tabatha started to thumb through the drawers. "That drawer is full of stuff. I don't believe this. What is this, Bruce?"

Bruce took a quick look. "Firearms, and a large sack of drugs in the back of this one. Hang on there. I'm going to put the drugs and the firearms in the safe. If they don't know the numbers they won't get them just yet." He closed the safe.

"We're in trouble, Bruce, I can hear a car."

"Move it, let's get out!"

"Let me neaten this stuff up so it doesn't look as if we were here."

"Just get out. Those guys will make a bigger mess than us, believe me."

Stumbling over one another, Bruce's phone rang. "Not now!" He flipped the lid to keep it quiet. "I'll get that later."

"Those guys stopped. They must have heard your phone."

"They haven't even gotten into the house, yet."

"Believe me, it isn't hard to hear through these walls. The house is so old I doubt it was never insulated so you can hear everything inside and out."

"Don't you have a land line in your house?"

"Of course."

"They'll think that's what they heard. Let's get out of here now!"

"I'm coming."

Both Bruce and Tabatha made it through the side door. Tabatha tripped, stumbling down the stairs into the tall grass. "Don't get up Tabatha, stay low in the grass with me."

"That hurt."

"Don't say anything or they will hear us."

Tabatha whispered, "Why don't you go, get away from here? If they find me, they at least know who I am. I can give them some kind of excuse for being around the house."

"Sorry, they'll kidnap you, I'm not leaving you here. We'll lie still until you can move. You're coming with me. I'm taking no chances."

"Look Bruce, you can see just a little into that window if you lift your head a bit. They're in the back room."

"Do you know who they are?"

"George is the bald one with the scar and the black beard and Sam is the blonde one."

Bruce and Tabatha watched as the men continued to toss furniture around.

"Come Tabatha, they won't hear us over the noise they're making. They're too busy trying to find Bill's stash." He pulled Tabatha up, "Can you walk? Did you break your ankle?"

Tabatha pulled back, "Let's listen for another minute." It was easy to hear their conversation.

"Ann must have confiscated those documents, George."

"Could be Bill hid them knowing we would come for them. He wouldn't have wanted to take the chance of those names getting into the cop's hands or even ours, knowing him."

"I'll get them somehow but the plan is, we first grab Tabatha and then we get Ann and this time we force her, threaten her, to tell us were Bill kept everything. Let's look in the closet. Here's another room? A safe, do you know the combination?"

"No, I don't George, but please slow down. You want to be caught for kidnapping? You've got to stop this carry on. You'll get us both killed."

"What are you saying, Sam? You know you are an accomplice. You've been with me all the way."

"You don't seem to care, but I do know that. We could get a few years for burglary but kidnapping? Murder is the death penalty. Don't you get it George?"

"We need the money. I didn't think Bill had the smarts to have hidden the money that well."

"I guess if he couldn't keep it, he wouldn't let us get our hands on it. That surprises me, I always thought he was nothing but a drunk."

"He fooled us both, man."

"Ann might know about that."

Then the voices faded.

"Let's get out of here, Tabatha. Can you stand up?"

"But those men?"

"They left. Look over there, the car is pulling out of the driveway."

"The house was left in a mess, Bruce."

"It doesn't matter. Let's get us out of here, now!"

Chapter Forty-One
The Documents

"You have to come with me Tabatha. Can you walk?"

"I'm all right. I don't think I sprained anything."

"Come, get in my car and we'll get away from here."

Bruce asked, "Did you recognize the car?"

"That's the same car that always comes to the house."

"I need to take you to a safe location after this."

"Commit me to foster care? How can you? I've trusted you all the way and now you want to send me away."

"I'm not going to do that. How can I let you go back to that house? You can stay at my house."

"I think I need to go back to my house. I need to straighten up what George and Sam pulled apart in the house so that my Mom doesn't see any of that."

"Then I have to come with you."

"If you do, we need an excuse to tell Ann when she finds you with me. She'll accuse you of stealing everything. How will she know any different?"

"Before we do that, we need to take what you have and see if it is all that you need to identify your existence."

"Where to?"

"We hit the Coffee Shop scene."

"Okay. You have my cup already."

"I didn't bring that with me, but that won't matter."

"You can't keep buying me more cups."

"Don't worry about that. Let's go check these papers out."

It wasn't but a few short minutes, driving up to the local coffee shop. With papers spread across a table, they began to examine them.

"Look, here's a picture of you and a document. It says your name is Tabatha Rosander. Isn't that the name you are going by?"

"I am."

"How about that, it says you are a year old in this picture. It has to be your birthdate because you're blowing the candles out on that cake. Look at the background, it looks almost like a bar."

"That is my birthdate all right and here look, a notarized copy to verify my birth. At least I've been led to believe it is mine. That's all there is about me. It still doesn't tell me who I am."

"At least we know for sure you are Tabatha Rosander. If I'm not mistaken, your surname is Swedish. Actually both your first and last name seem to be Swedish." Bruce hesitated for a bit, "I have connections and I can get this all sorted out for you if you would allow me to introduce you to an investigator."

"If I do that, what happens to me?"

Before they realized it, Marybeth showed up with a few friends at the coffee shop.

"Oh no, not Marybeth, again. I don't want to see her. She told me my Dad was in jail before I ever knew about it."

True to life, Marybeth was with her friends. It seemed she wasn't about to miss her opportunity with new news she had just acquired. "Hey, Tabatha, did you know that Bruce, the guy you are with right now, is not really a student at Melville? He's not a kid like us, he just pretends to be."

"What are you talking about Marybeth?"

"You know my cousin, Laura. Well, she asked her Mom why the handsomest kid in the school couldn't date her? Why was Bruce interested in you, of all people and then from the other side of town? Well, guess what? Her mother, and like I already said, my Aunt, told us not to say anything, but I knew you should know that Bruce really isn't a student at all. You've trusted the wrong guy!"

Tabatha was stunned. She turned to face Bruce, asking as her voice trembled, "What's going on? Why don't I know who you are? Tell me now, who are you?"

"Tabatha, she's just jealous but stand with me. If you want to hate me, you can. You must let me get you through this. You can't do it by yourself, please. I know what I'm talking about. You are too smart to jump at what jealous kids are talking about. They will gossip till they drop just because things aren't going their way. You don't have to like me and slap me in the face if you like, I don't care, but let's just get through this situation. I have an explanation and when you are safe, and then, if you wish, I'll be gone."

"I don't know what to say, and then you turn out to be a safe cracker! I'm too weak to even argue. I think I don't care who you are but please, I don't want to be sold." Tabatha stood up for a moment, "I have to go for a walk. I don't know what to think now."

Bruce followed her, "Please Tabatha, I'm not going to let you go. Please don't make me take you into custody for your own sake."

"I get it, now you are a police officer?"

"I'm undercover to save your life. In a nutshell, we are after George and Sam but they are holding you and Ann hostage."

Tabatha leaned against a lamp pole at the side of the road. "So now I go into foster care anyhow?"

"I don't want to do that but you and I heard those men at your house. This is real life and you have to let me help you so that we can solve this once and for all. You two aren't the only ones he is holding hostage."

"Where to from here, Bruce? What do you want me to do?" Tabatha hesitated for a moment, "My common sense says, I should run for my life just as I planned all along but my head says stop and God says be still."

"Tabatha, God has to win out."

"I don't know where I'd be without him. Please help me but don't you be a kidnapper. I've already been kidnapped once."

"Abducted. I promise, I'm not a kidnapper. Let me show you my badge. Take a good look, read it. I'm here to help. Let's go back into the coffee shop."

"Okay, I guess. Why would you care about me, though?"

"That part will come out in the end but meanwhile you are in my trust, you are my charge. I have to be sure you are safe."

They sat there for a moment looking at one another but Tabatha had that *I'm going to die look.* "Bruce I have to get back to the house with this *stash."* She handed Bruce the money. "I have to put it back and then straighten Ann's house up so she doesn't catch on that they've already been through all her stuff?"

"Okay, but we won't put the money back just yet. If George and Sam get it, Ann won't have anything left. I think Ann doesn't know about the money. She doesn't even know that Bill had it stashed in the house. Let's keep it that way. Here's the deal, you are not going in alone. I'm coming."

"What if they catch us this time?"

"I call in help."

"I guess. You are a Police Officer."

"Undercover investigator."

Tabatha didn't know that Smith was listening in the far corner of the coffee shop. He needed to be totally aware of what was about to go down.

Bruce motioned for Smith to join them. "Tabatha, you need to meet Sergeant Smith. We are in on all of what you are going through. We wanted you to be able to graduate and get the scholarship. We also, didn't want to take the chance to allow you to get hurt. You and I will go to your house. Put things in order. They couldn't find anything they wanted because you already had it before George and Sam got there."

"Oh, but they will. They will try to force Ann to open the safe and we already know she can't do that so then they'll shoot it open. Who knows what they'll do to Ann. I doubt that Bill would have let her in on the *drug pushing*, but they said their *clients' names* are in there. That I heard when I stumbled in the grass by the stairs with you."

"Then Bruce," Smith continued, "you must go with Tabatha. Do you think you can open the safe?"

"I already have. Here's the stuff we got and I put the other stuff in the safe."

"Do you think you can get those files?"

"Probably if we can be fast enough."

"We'll have Steve set up a *look out* for us."

"But I have to live there. I have to sleep in that house tonight." Tabatha insisted.

Smith and Bruce both looked at one another. "It could work, Bruce if you get out of there with the files quickly enough. We don't need but one or two, leave the others for further evidence."

"That might be too dangerous for her."

"Don't worry about me, Bruce. I have your phone with me."

Bruce asked, "When does Ann get home?"

"Usually pretty late."

"Wouldn't George and Sam find her at the Bar?"

"They'd never do that. The bar doesn't know their business and they want to keep it that way."

"Ann should be safe until she arrives home at least."

"I don't think they'll do anything while I'm around."

"Don't be so sure, Tabatha. They've already threatened and probably are desperate now."

Tabatha and Bruce tried every door and searched every room in the house. Tabatha wanted to be sure she wouldn't be jumped on. "The coast is clear, Bruce."

"Let's just straighten everything up and then you can leave. You can have what files you need from the cabinet."

"I just needed a few of the buyers and maybe suppliers." He took a batch of files under his arm. "There, that'll do it. Let's go catch up with Sergeant Smith."

Tabatha had managed to straighten the house so that Ann wouldn't know what had just happened. Everything looked undisturbed.

"Shouldn't you take the firearms with you?"

"No, that could be the evidence we need later. I just didn't want them to have it quite so easily. I need to get them stalled out for a bit but there has to be a proper investigation. If I disturb all the evidence I could do more harm than good. I'll just take some of the files for now. That has to be enough."

"I really have to wait here until Ann gets home."

"I'm afraid for you. You know if anything goes wrong I will be to blame for it."

"Tonight, I'll be fine. I have your phone and all I have to do is hit the redial button."

"If Sergeant Smith doesn't think this is a good idea, he may be back to get you."

"Please don't take me into custody."

"If you come with me, you can stay at my place. I'll even have a lady cop stay with you, if you wish."

"I have to stay here otherwise Ann will be worried that I didn't get back. She would have to tell George and Sam that I went missing. You know what that means."

"That could all be resolved as well. I'll let you stay but you have to call if anything happens. I mean anything. If you don't, we come for you, no matter what."

"I know, already. I'll be okay and I think I know what I'm doing."

"Remember, it's the *outfield* unless you call. I'll get to wherever you are as quickly as possible. I still feel you shouldn't stay here anymore."

"Bruce, please, I'll see you in the *outfield!*"

Chapter Forty-Two
The Set Up

Tabatha could feel the cold sweat on her hands. She was freezing with fear but maybe it was the house that made her cold on this warm humid early summer evening. The sound of the TV was at a whisper because Tabatha wanted to hear everything around her. She took comfort in knowing they had checked all the rooms before Bruce left to be sure there was no one hiding anywhere. The house was *certified empty*. It had to be. Still every noise in the old decrepit structure made Tabatha tremble.

Then a car pulled up to the house. *Please, Lord, don't let it be George or Sam.* Still shaking Tabatha dared to glance out the window. There weren't any more choices. She might as well prepare herself for she feared the worst. Lifting the curtain an inch or so to keep from being seen, Tabatha gave a sigh of relief seeing her mother alone. She crumbled on the sofa waiting for her mother to come in.

"Hi, Mom, how was your day? I hope you aren't too tired from working so long."

"I'm getting tired of being a bar maid. This was never what I wanted to do."

"And then you had me. That's why you are working in the bar, right?"

"Not really and that isn't how it was supposed to go, I just don't have the guts to make it any different."

"If it's any comfort to you, when I get a real job, I plan to take care of you. I've taken so much of your life."

"That's just not so, Tabatha, you would have been my first priority no matter what and you have been my reason to carry on. You are not the reason I'm in this fix."

"Then why?"

"I'm just too weak to fight but enough of that, Tabatha."

Tabatha knew the conversation was over. No more questions, no matter what.

"Have you applied to any Colleges yet?"

"Not yet, but that's the next thing I will do. I have to do it before school locks down for the summer so I can use their computer."

"Why don't you hang out at the local library? They have computers you can use."

"Thanks, I'll do that tomorrow. I don't know why I didn't think of that. I had to get special permission to use the school and I can only do that while the teachers are finishing up."

"That way you don't have to be here in the house. Why don't you leave early? Do you know when they open?"

"I don't but I'm meeting Bruce in the *outfield* at school so then I'll go there after that. Yeah, I'll leave early, I can do that."

"It sounds as if Bruce has turned out to be your safety net. Is he all that I wish him to be for you?"

"I don't think we're an *item*, but he turned out to be my *helper.*"

"I just pray that you stay safe, that's all that I ever wanted for you." Ann sounded exhausted. "By the way, are you feeling any better? I totally forgot that you should've been home all week."

"Don't worry about that, I have so many instructors that none of them really get involved. The principal and the nurse knew I would be back if I was better."

Ann turned the TV volume up as they sat there. Both sat silently, staring at the TV while their minds were in a world of their own.

"It is time for me to hit the sack, Mom."

"Can't you stay just a bit longer with me? You look very tired yourself, like something has happened to you?"

"I guess I'm still tired from not feeling well before but a night of sleep should cure that. Do you want to talk about something I need to know, maybe?"

"Oh, no, I just don't seem to get to talk with you since I've been working so much."

"Have you heard from Bill?"

"I'm going to see him tomorrow sometime. I have stuff to ask him."

"If you're going to see him, where exactly is he?"

"A business venture, he should be gone about a year."

"If he's on a business venture, where is it you are going to see him, maybe I could go with you to visit with him?"

"I don't think that would be wise. Like I said, I don't want you around any of those guys."

"Almost forgot, *he's only a make believe father,* right?"

"You don't forget, do you? I do want you to remember that."

"So maybe I should tell you, Marybeth at school already told me."

"Then you know."

"I do."

"I wanted everything to be as normal as possible. Then you know why I want you at the library until I get home. You could call the bar before you come home to be sure I'm here."

The house was quiet now but sleep wasn't coming any too easily. Tabatha tossed a good bit of the night. It wasn't any wonder because she already knew that the awfulness of the future was uncertain. She couldn't let her mother stay while she went off to college. It had become evident that George and Sam were up to no good. Maybe Bruce would be able to advise. He was in Law Enforcement and seemed to be very wise in all the times they were able to share together. She could need his help and he had left her with his cell phone. Still, she tossed until the early hours of the morning.

Tabatha was too tired to remember when she dozed off but now her alarm went off and that meant she needed to quickly shower and be out of the house. *Yesterday, now I remember. I need to get out of here.* Just as soon as Tabatha turned off the shower, she could hear the conversation below her in the house.

"Just stop it. I'm going to see Bill today and will find out where he stashed the money."

"We'll blow the safe open and find the stuff for ourselves. Just bring Tabatha down. If you don't we will go up and get her!"

Now for certain Tabatha knew she needed to find a way out of the house. She needed a way to escape and that wasn't going to be easy. *I'll put the shower tap back on while I get dressed. Hopefully they'll think I'm busy.* Within minutes she was ready but she kept the tap running and dialed Bruce. She waited, but there was no answer.

Chapter Forty-Three
The Escape

Bruce was in charge of the debriefing lecture for the Monday morning meeting at the police station. It was his assignment to give instructions for the procedures of the day. It was a necessary part of their work to enable the officers to fulfill their duties more easily. It was where they would be informed of what might be going down with assignments given that where essential. Not yet finished with the lecture, his phone rang. Bruce knew it would be another ten minutes before he would be done but he had to grab it.

Bruce could feel his heart sink, it was too late, Tabatha had already hung up. In a panicky state, Bruce turned to Sergeant Smith, "Take over, I've got to go." He held his phone tightly as though he wanted it to ring one more time.

Sergeant Smith turned to the men, "Looks like we have a situation going down. Officers, you are dismissed. Be listening for your code we will quite probably need back-up." He sounded urgent.

"What do I do, Smith? Can't call her back if she's in trouble. Having the phone ring could cause her circumstances to escalate. I have to go."

"Where do we find you and Tabatha, on the Outfield?"

"Her house. She wouldn't have called except that she has a problem leaving her house."

Smith was calling the shots, "I'm going with you. Steve, bring Atlas, we're going to need him. These guys are armed and dangerous but remember, we have to first rescue Tabatha. No shooting until we have her safe."

"What? Why did you let her go back to the house? Even I knew this was going to happen. Now we are going to have a hostage situation and that means someone gets killed. I understand you wanted to get the whole gang, but at the expense of a young innocent, defenseless gal? That just doesn't make any sense." Steve was obviously disgusted.

Smith ignored Steve. He knew what had to be done and he knew this was the best way they could do it. They needed to take a murderer off the streets. It would work if everyone kept their cool and proceeded exactly as planned. He knew they would be able to get all of them.

Steve continued complaining, "A shoot out wouldn't matter if we had pulled out Tabatha. Now you know we're going to face a hostage situation all because you wanted to catch the gang members. I don't get it."

"Shut up and bring Atlas, we're going to need him now. Keep your sirens off."

They sped toward the house.

He's not answering. Tabatha checked the window. *If I jump, I'll break a bone and with my luck, I'll break my neck. On top of that, I would never be able to out run them. I'm not that good at shimming down drain pipes! Lord please, I need your help.* She tried her phone one more time.

"Tabatha is that you? What's going on? Where are you?"

"Bruce, I heard them say they are taking me away, they want me. What do I do?"

"Can you stay in your room?"

"They said they were coming up to get me if Ann didn't call me down. My door is locked but they'll break it down quite easily, it's just made of thin plywood, and then what do I do?"

"I don't want a shoot-out. Is there any way you can safely get out?"

"I'm afraid to try the drain pipes. Don't know if I can make it."

"Don't do that just yet."

There was obvious hesitation on the line with Tabatha.

"Talk to me Tabatha."

"What do I do, Bruce? Maybe I can try to sneak down and try for the side door. I can hear the men yelling at the top of their lungs. If they spot me, they'll grab me. Help me, please!"

Bruce could hear Tabatha's desperation. "We'll grab you when you come through the door. Stall a minute. We are almost at your house, about half block away."

"But, I'll be trapped if I don't get out of this room before they come up. They'll hold me hostage and you know what that means. I have to get out of here. I'm going down." Tabatha was quiet for the moment.

Suddenly the phone slammed closed.

"Let her try to get out first, Bruce. If she can, it will be the best we can ask for." Smith was experienced and this seemed the best way for the moment.

I'll just run for my life. Tabatha tripped over her feet coming down the stairs. She quickly looked and realized the men were facing the other way. She slipping behind Ann, grabbing the door for the escape while they were busy grumbling to one another. Ann gave Tabatha a shove, pushing her through the door. Tabatha made a run for it.

George heard the scuffle and turned when he saw Tabatha disappear through the door. Shoving Ann out of the way, he shouted, "Where do you think you're going, kid?" He began to run after her.

As quickly as she could Tabatha ran down the cluttered pathway. In her heart she knew she could never out run these men. She decided she would give it all she had to the death if it needed to be. With a dash, out of nowhere it seemed, Atlas, the large police dog dove between the men. Both George and Sam stopped, standing dead in their tracks. Atlas had their attention. They could see his front teeth as he growling at them, awaiting a command to proceed from his master.

Tabatha was about to turn toward the high school, wanting to make a mad dash when she spotted Bruce's car. The door flung open and she stumbled in.

"Are you okay?"

Tabatha was gasping. "That wasn't easy. What now? Where do I go? I didn't exactly anticipate this. I just thought I could disappear and find my own way. I didn't know George had a leash on me."

Chapter Forty-Four
End of the Row

Ann locked up the house and drove away in her car. She would drive around and see if she could follow them should they be successful in their pursuit. She gave a sigh of relief when she saw the car stop with the police dog as he darted after George and Sam. *I just knew I had seen Bruce before. He's an undercover police officer. He's been in the Bar.* That settled, she drove to work knowing neither one of the men would come for her there. She would be safe for the day.

George was totally disgusted that they had failed in the attempt to keep Tabatha in their clutches. It was still in the early hours of the morning while the sun could barely be seen coming up on the horizon.

"Dog or no dog, Sam, you were supposed to run interference between the dog and Tabatha. I could have grabbed her easily grabbed her. That's what I've been paying you for all this time."

"And get bit? I want my arm, man!"

"We'd at least have Tabatha. No one even knew she existed until now. She was our perfect plan, our perfect get-a-way, and our hostage to get out of all this."

"The cops have a lead on us. They've figured it out." George went to return to the house, "Ann locked up the house and took off."

"That never stopped us before."

"Don't forget that Ann is going to see Bill. She'll find out the combination and before she starts to open up the safe, we'll be right behind her. She's not going to run off with anything."

"You'd better get all the information you can before you do something stupid. Without her we are at square one. She doesn't talk, we have nothing."

"We can always blow the safe apart. We don't really need her anymore and it wasn't she we wanted in the first place. Tabatha was supposed to be our ticket back into freedom."

"We can always find Jane at the Bar."

"We can't go there, Sam. If you say the cops are onto us, they swarm that place and then it's done for us. I say we wait until she comes home tonight."

They both sped off in a hurry. "We have to stay out of sight, Sam."

"I say take off and save our own skin."

"Can't leave without the money. We're broke, we have to get that money Bill stashed."

"We're risking getting caught, George."

"Here's my plan. First make her give us those files and money. Set the house on fire with Ann tied up in. Then we'll be gone before they get the fire out. Go back to Mexico."

"That will be murder."

"They'll never find us and by the time they are looking for us, we are gone."

"Then when we get caught it'll be the death penalty. George, you are not thinking logically, that's just being stupid. Let Ann go, just take the money and the dealer names then make a *bee line* out of here."

"We can't do that. If Ann doesn't talk, Tabatha will."

"Got a better idea, George?"

"Do as I say, you heard my plan or it'll be over for you too."

"Just let it go. Take what money we came for and disappear. When Bill gets out of jail, we'll be back and make him hand over the stash."

"Need all of that stuff or we'll be implicated anyhow. Have to get it, that's my plan. Nothing else will do, I'm going for all or nothing. Anything they get will be over my dead body."

"Are you sure you want to take the rap?"

"If we destroy the evidence, they'll never nail it on us."

"I don't like it, George. You're destroying your alibi. Wasn't Ann going to be your alibi should you need one? What's more, I'm not going to get caught on attempted kidnapping, or murder with you. If that's what you want to get hung on, that's your choice, not mine."

"Are you bailing on me?"

"Unless you start talking sense."

"Nobody bails on me."

"It's your fault that Bill got hung on that charge of bank robbery. You didn't need to rob that bank. It was just senseless."

"He was nothing but a drunk. Said something like he couldn't do this anymore, couldn't live with himself anymore. I didn't need that. It had to be done."

"Let's go and wait where we can watch for Ann to get home."

Sam started the car as George jumped in. "Where to George? We need to do our own stake out until she gets in there."

They drove off into the nearby park. Sam walked off to the hot dog stand to get grub for himself. George sat there waiting to see if they had been followed. *Why hadn't the cops come after him? They knew full well that Tabatha had run from them. My only chance is to wait for Ann to get back tonight and go on with my plan. I'll deal with Sam later. I need him for a cover for now, I'll make him take the blame for this one. He's going as soft as Bill. He'll be my next scape-goat.*

They spent a few hours sitting in the nearby park keeping an eye on the house. It was already getting late and they hadn't seen any sign of Ann.

"Let's go into the house, and break into the safe without her."

"How do you plan to do that?"

"Bill should have left the firearms in a desk. When he first moved into the house, he showed me where they were. Let's go for it. We need them to blow the safe open anyhow."

With no one home, they found the hidden room, pushed the door open and looked everywhere. "Weird, they aren't here anymore. I was sure, Sam, this was the place."

"I thought you always carry a gun. You're armed aren't you?"

"I'll try but these bullets might rick-a-shay, so watch out. Let's do it."

It took a few bullets to blast the lock off. "Okay, let's pull out everything in there."

"Where's the money, Sam? Who took the money?" George was angry enough to shoot anyone in sight. "Where did Bill hide the money then?"

"Should've waited for Ann to come back from seeing Bill with the information."

"Bill tricked us. I thought he was nothing but a drunk."

"George, I found the ledger with all the entries. Some files of names with leads but I know these are not all of them. Where are the rest?"

George grabbed the files. "Where's Tabatha's file? I had Bill put that in this cabinet and somebody removed it."

"Are you really sure? They've lived here five years already. It might be in another corner or maybe Ann needed it for her school and just forgot to put it back?"

"You saw when we went in the house the other day, we couldn't find anything. We didn't even see the door to this room."

"They use the door as a wall."

"George, that was meant to be a hidden room. At one time this area was a very prestigious location. People of influence lived here. Did you ever find who's house it was in the past?"

"It was of no interest to me. Cheap is all I needed. It had a maid's quarters and that was what made it good for Tabatha. It horrifies me that she got away. If I had known that, she would never have had her freedom."

"I don't think, George, we would have gotten away with that. That's exactly what they had on the news reports when we first took possession of her. They were looking for two men and a baby. Remember?"

They both stood looking at one another. There was no money to find. "Ann has to know where it is. Bill would have told her especially if he didn't leave it where it should have been."

"If Ann can't produce the money, I say we tie up Ann and burn down the house."

"George, I already told you, I'm not going to be your alibi on this one. I don't think we are on the same page anymore. I'm asking you not to harm Ann."

"Sam, I've had just about enough from you. If we get rid of Ann, Tabatha will be ours. She has nowhere to go for very long. Eventually Tabatha will be out in the open again. We'll be watching for her."

"Look, I found the bag of packaged drugs. We can sell them ourselves for a while and get money from that. I suggest we just take them and get out of here. Anything more we do, it'll be curtains for us." George was seething, his anger wouldn't let up. "Let's break for coffee at the local coffee shop. They don't know us there, so we can sit down and talk through all our scenarios. Make some wise decisions for a change. If I'm to be your bodyguard, do this my way."

"I'll do it your way only if I can find Tabatha. I want that gal to go with us."

"You're just kidding yourself, George. The cops are on to us."

"What makes you come up with that conclusion, Sam?"

"How do you think Tabatha got away?"

"It was because of that idiot dog and her friend. You should have gone after her."

"Come on George, that was a police dog waiting for the command to pull us down. It doesn't matter anymore, there is no way we can take Tabatha."

"Sam, the cops can't know who she is. They'll let her go because she can't prove her existence. They'll think she's Ann's daughter, the school will back that up from her registration."

"Don't you think they can figure it out?"

"How? She has no paperwork, she's not even a legal citizen. Can't stay in hiding for too long. Think about it Sam, how did we get to keep Tabatha all these years without intervention from anyone before? She might have a friend or two but nobody's looking for her anymore. She'll stay with a friend and that's where we step in and find her."

"You don't have to be a *rocket scientist* to know the cops are already on our tail. If we don't disappear, we're done."

"I've come this far and I'm telling you, you're not bailing on me."

"Oh yeah?"

George pulled his gun and started pistol-whipping Sam.

"If you're so tough why don't you just shoot me? See where that will get you. Who will you blame for my dead body? Bill has an alibi already, remember, he's locked up. Can't use that excuse, can you?"

"Get up off the ground. Ann's driving up the driveway. Let's go."

"Let her at least get settled. Give her a couple of hours. She went to see Bill so we might very well have everything we need."

"We'll see."

"You try one more murder and I'm history."

"Oh yeah, Sam, you had better be on my side."

"Sorry Buddy, if that's the way you think, I'm out of here. See you at the coffee shop."

Sam walked away.

Chapter Forty-Five
Nearing the Goal

Anita and Dr. Tim Turner were in their guarded room and had been there for a solid week waiting for news. All they were able to do was use room service as they continued to wait.

"When can we find Tabatha? I just don't get it, how long have we waited?"

"I don't think it will be much longer. Apparently something was going down at the school we were at. They couldn't allow us to go in or anyone else for that matter. You saw the students exiting while the place was surrounding with cops."

"We've been listening to the news on TV every day but I haven't heard anything."

"Probably because they were able to contain everything. Remember, that wasn't in the best part of town. Could be things happen there more as a routine and unless someone gets hurt, there is no news to report. You know we very well could have gotten into the middle of all that and even been the cause of a gun battle."

"I just get tired of waiting. I'm not good at that. Remember it's been sixteen years for me."

Day after day, they sat there with just the TV, the local newspaper and themselves. Anita had hung onto a few crossword puzzles to amuse herself while Tim worked on his Medical assignments he had brought with him. He stayed in touch with the Shelter and the Hospital. From time to time he would take calls that came in for him to make major decisions.

The phone rang but it was for Tim. "Okay, I will. I will tell Anita that you asked. Just as soon as we know anything, we'll let you know. Thank you."

"The Shelter was interested to know if we had found your daughter. Well, you heard what I said."

They talked sometime about the times they had together at the Shelter while Anita regained her strength.

The phone began ringing again, Tim answered. "Hello. Okay you are saying we can come down? It won't take long for us to get ready." Tim turned toward Anita, "How long before you are ready?"

"Give me ten."

Tim and Anita were at the registrar's desk in less time than they expected. Office Turner's broad smile was a dead give-away.

"Okay, people, you don't have to stay at your hotel anymore. We will take you to a meeting place and brief you on the information we have."

"You mean you want us to pack our stuff up now?"

"No, I mean you are no longer under house arrest. We can go."

"You found Tabatha?"

"The plan is to take you to a meeting place."

"Does she know we are here?"

Tim was insistent. "Are you saying you know where Tabatha is, then?"

"Just come with me."

Anita was feeling uneasy about everything. She knew that if the man called George was to see her now, he would likely stop and accuse her of smuggling drugs across the border from Mexico into the United States. He would tell how they met and then she would have to stand trial. That was not her plan. She merely wanted to find her daughter. For her this could mean probation time in the very least, if not jail time and then deportation. Would Tim stand by her even in this situation? There was no doubt in her mind that both Sam and George would recognize her. If being in house arrest was to be a taste of the rest of her life, then she felt just maybe she had been prepared. After sixteen years of absence from her daughter's life how could she expect anything from Tabatha? Tabatha couldn't know her struggles for life let alone how to find her. Then maybe this meeting they were to have would be fruitless anyhow. Maybe they would just let her down easily and it would all be over. All this struggle would be for nothing.

Anita wanted to know, "Are the kidnappers going to be in there to accuse me?"

"That wasn't the plan. They aren't aware of what we are doing, so I would say no. You have nothing to concern yourself about. We aren't going for a confession. We are going to meet for a reunion with your daughter. How does that sound?"

"Good, but I'm excited and scared all at the same time. Can you tell me anything about Tabatha? Was she involved in drugs and stuff like that?"

"Was she a good girl? Is that what you are asking?"

"I guess."

"I can tell you some of the situation. She attended church."

"She did?"

"Yes, she did. No, the lady that took care of her is a widow who was married to a cop. Her name is Ann, but not even Tabatha knows that just yet. That will all come out in the wash when we meet together. You have to know that Tabatha knows nothing. She has no idea that she has a mother. She found out only recently that Ann was not her mother. She is quite probably in total shock already."

Tim asked, "Is it good for us to be in the picture for her, then?"

"I think it is. You might also want to know she graduated with a four-year scholarship for the College of her choice. She is a very bright gal. She was very studious. You should be very proud of her. Ann did a very good job. You will have no regrets."

Tim continued, "We are going to have to help this lady you call Ann. If she could do that then I would say, God knew how to take care of Tabatha."

"That's just about all I remember. I remember pleading with God to please take care of Tabatha. I didn't deserve anything, but she certainly did and I didn't want her to be paying for what I did. Though, when I think about it, she payed dearly. I really hope I can make it up to her. She deserves more than I can give her."

"Let's get going, okay?"

Chapter Forty-Six
The Story

Tabatha was trembling. All she could say, "What happens to Ann? They'll kill her. They don't need her anymore."

"Just come with me. You remember Smith you met the other day, he will be meeting us there as well, it'll give you a chance to catch your breath and give us a chance to go over what has to happen next to keeping you safe." Driving back to the coffee shop, Bruce wanted to make a note of all that had just happened.

Steve drove up as well with Atlas in tow.

However, as Tabatha and Bruce entered the Coffee house, Tabatha couldn't believe her eyes. In a whisper, "I have to get out of here, Bruce."

"Why?"

"You see what I see? George and Sam are at the counter. Look outside, there's that black Camaro in the corner of the parking lot. That has to be them."

Tabatha stood behind Bruce and Steve, petting Atlas, hoping not to be seen.

"Listen. Just listen to them."

The Barista started a conversation with the guys as they placed their orders. "By the way, guys, I don't remember seeing you here before, business in town?"

"Yeah, you might say that."

"From around here?"

"Can't say that I am. My buddy here, George, he attended Melville High many years ago. Says he knows every nook and cranny in this town."

"Oh, when did you graduate, George?"

Laughing, "George didn't. He found a better way to make a living, didn't you George?"

"Stay out of my personal life. It isn't your business."

"I think you've made it my business by now."

It looked as if the light went on with George when he turned, he saw Tabatha standing behind Bruce. "Hey kid" Tabatha didn't respond. "I'm talking to you, kid."

Bruce looked up at George. "And what were you wanting to say to this young lady?"

"Shut up, George. She's not your problem anymore." Sam saw what was about to erupt.

"Grab her, Sam. She's who we came for, she belongs to me. Grab her."

Sam hesitated. This was a public place of business. He didn't intend to get caught kidnapping much less being involved with a hostage takeover.

Bruce put out his hand to keep them at bay from Tabatha. "Back off man if you know what's good for you."

George tried to push Bruce aside. "If you know what's good for you, see this?" George pulled his gun out for everyone to see.

There wasn't a Barista to be seen, they were on the floor.

"George, stop it, you're crazy, man. You're about to blow the biggest deal of our lives!"

"Not so fast, man." Bruce and Steve stood between them and Tabatha.

George didn't recognize Bruce and Steve as undercover cops and had no intention to obey, "Stand back everyone. If anyone makes a sound or calls the cops, I'll start shooting. This is not the first time I've killed anyone."

"George, now you're kidnapping. When you take Tabatha you become a kidnapper." Sam didn't want any part of this holdup.

"Taking Tabatha isn't kidnapping. She belongs to us more than she ever did to Bill and Ann."

"Excuse me, George, you're saying taking Tabatha isn't kidnapping? Just how do you figure that? Tell us how her parents died? You tell them, George. Do you have the guts to make your case?"

By now every undercover cop had surrounded the coffee shop just waiting for what was about to go down next.

"Get Tabatha in the car and shut up. Her parents were illegals, so who cared what happened to them. Even the cops would have cared less."

Smith wanted to hear the confessions. He was ready to identify himself.

"Tell them, George. How did they die?"

"Sure, I only shot Anton. Anita died of childbirth. She wouldn't have made it anyhow so I grabbed Tabatha. I saved her life. She would have starved alone in the desert."

"And what else did you manage to rip off?"

"They were dead. What did it matter? Why would I leave anything in the desert?"

"That was no rescue. Border Patrol was on our case so you couldn't leave them alone, you had to kill."

"They were worthless druggies. They would've been caught anyhow because both of them were transporting drugs across the border as well and Tabatha would have been deported. But instead I gave Tabatha to Ann to care for."

"Tell me, what do you want to do with Tabatha?" asked Bruce.

"George thinks he can get money for her. I told him I would have no part of his plan this time. He has already threatened me."

George ignored Sam and continued, "Tabatha's just a kid isn't she? She belongs to no one."

"I wouldn't exactly say that. She has her rights because from what I saw on her birth certificate it says she was born in the US."

"I'm telling you, she has no birth certificate!"

"Oh yes she does. We do know her story and we were able to put the pieces together, so drop that gun now!" Sergeant Smith had his gun drawn.

"Sam, grab Tabatha and let's get out of here. Take her hostage. Take her to the car and shut up."

George gave a loud shout, "Get out of here and in the car Tabatha!"

That was about it with Tabatha. She hadn't forgotten the gun pointing into the lobby. "Who do you think you are? I'm not your dog! Shoot everyone in this place but you ain't taking me hostage." She knew very well her life would be worthless should happen. She wasn't about to comply. What good was it to stay alive and be sold as a prostitute anyhow? She had been left alone until now and she had decided that submitting to these men would not be in her future.

Sam and George looked at one another, startled. They had never heard a peep out of Tabatha in the past.

"I'm not with you, George. I can't do that. You are on your own now."

"You two are not going anywhere. Put your gun down!" Demanded Bruce.

Chapter Forty-Seven
The Fire

The coffee shop door flung open. An officer stood in the doorway, "I need to find Tabatha. Is Tabatha here?"

Tabatha bolted out, "Sir?"

"Your house is on fire. We have to know where to find Ann."

Tabatha turned to glare at Sam and George, "You killed her."

Looking at George, Sam answered, "Tell me you didn't do that?"

What did you say, Sam?" Bruce wanted answers.

"Ann could be in there." Sam was seriously concerned. He didn't want to be part of a murder either.

Tabatha pushed the officer out of her pathway, "Let me go help her. I have to help her. Please!"

George wielded his gun around, "Don't anyone move!" Tabatha couldn't be stopped, gun or not she tore out of the building to get to where Ann might be.

Sam shouted, "Don't do it, George. Put that gun down. You'll get the death penalty for this. Kidnapping is bad enough. It's over, man."

George wielded his 38 toward Sam. This time he wasn't about to hesitate. He'd been on the run for years and in his mind, the only way of escape was to kill those around him. This time it was only one shot and Sam slumped to the floor. Atlas jumped, dragging George down. A scuffle ensued but Sergeant Smith grabbed one of George's arm while Bruce pulled his gun from his clutches. They both had been well trained for just such an emergency. In seconds all two of the men had ben cuffed.

"We need the paramedics. This man is still breathing."

"Just help me, please. I will tell you everything you need to know. I never wanted to be a part of George's schemes. He blackmailed me."

George began cussing.

"Tape his mouth, he's nothing but a rotten murderer." Sam gasped for air as the paramedics put the oxygen mask on him.

"Stay with us, Sam. Don't pass out on us." The paramedics worked exhaustingly to stop the bleeding.

Sam was wheeled into the emergency transport.

"Stay with him Steve." Atlas followed. "Be alert for any information." It went unspoken, but they would need everything thing they could get.

"We are doing all that we can."

Tabatha ran as fast as she could, the distance wasn't far. Already she could see the flames pouring out of windows. Nearing the house, Tabatha made one more dash to get there. Then hesitated for a just a moment to gather strength and resolve to enter that house. She could feel the inferno flames blow in her face. Still, knowing Ann would still be in the house, she had to try. Someone had to.

"Stop!"

"Marybeth, let me go! What are you doing here at the house? Please go away, I just don't have time for you. I have to rescue Ann." Tabatha wouldn't be stopped.

Marybeth grabbed her arm again. "You can't go into that house." She pulled Tabatha with all she had. Tabatha screamed, "You're hurting me, let me go!"

Marybeth tackled Tabatha to the ground until she could no longer move. "You can't go in there. The fire is too fierce."

"I have to, Ann's in there."

"I won't let you." Marybeth held Tabatha down though both of them were petite women and slender, all of 100 pounds but the adrenalin flowed in their bodies. Tabatha knew she had to get in the burning house and Marybeth knew it would be the last time she would ever see Tabatha alive. "You can't, I can't let you die. You're going to die if you go in there!"

Sirens were loud amid the heat of the building as Bruce raced from his car to assist in stopping Tabatha.

"Bruce, please, I have to find Ann." Tabatha was insistent. "Oh God, we are too late." She trembled as Bruce and Marybeth hung on to her, both watching the fire's intensity.

"We're too late! Ann couldn't have had a chance. The fire would have been too violent."

Marybeth gave out a yell, "Look Tabatha! The side of the house, who is that?"

"A man pulling someone out, and look, she is still tied to a chair!" Almost in a cheer, both Tabatha and Bruce yelled out.

"Ann!"

Ann couldn't talk but her entire body was trembling as she lay there. The paramedics raced to her side. They untied the ropes and laid her flat on the ground, putting cold compresses on her face and body.

Bruce asked, "What happened? How did you get in there?"

The stranger answered, "I saw flames coming from this house. I knew it hadn't been abandoned because from time to time I would see a young lady come out of there and sometimes I would see cars come and go, often late in the night." He started staring at Tabatha, "You are that young lady."

"I am."

"My instinct told me someone could easily be in there. I got as close as I could when I heard someone cry for help. I called 911 then tried to enter the building when I saw the flames were so intense, I wanted to hesitate but then I saw a lady tied to a chair. I only had time to pull her and the chair out. The smoke and the flames were too much to do anything."

Sergeant Smith was already on the scene. "Ann will be okay, thanks to you, Sir, a neighbor's fast action has saved her life."

Lying on the stretcher, Ann moaned, "I have nothing now."

"Don't ever worry, I will take care of you."

"You have your own life, Tabatha. I refuse to stand in your way. You have a scholarship you must use. You don't need to be thinking about me. I didn't know your mother but knowing you all these years, I know I could never stand in your way."

"I don't have any other mother, Ann. You are all I know. I promise to do everything I can to take care of you."

"She'll be okay. Her vitals are good." The house was in ashes by now with hot embers scattered about. The paramedics worked with Ann transporting her to the hospital.

Tabatha was stunned. This was now reality. No mother, no father and now no family. *"Oh God, I've tied a knot in the rope and I'm hanging on. Help me to hold tight."*

It was as if Tabatha could hear God speak to her, *"Be still and know that I am God... I will never leave you, I will never forsake you."*

Tabatha and Marybeth sat on the ground, neither of them spoke.

Sergeant Smith and Bruce had left for the hospital so now only the firemen attempting to clean up the remains of the building. Some items like the bathroom and kitchen pictures lay about on the ground amide the smoldering ashes. The chair Ann had been tied up in, lay broken on the ground. Police were milling about the premise looking for clues as if they needed any. They already knew the reason but needed the exact location of where the fire was set.

"Nurse, can we talk to your patient? It is important to our investigation."

"We have him hooked up but I don't know what kind of response you will get. If the monitors show that your interrogation is causing physical stress you will have to leave."

"That's good enough for us, we will comply." Both, Nichols and Smith entered the room.

"Sam, can you hear us?"

"I can."

"We'll make a plea deal with you. You can have an attorney with you or talk with us now or later. Bruce read you your rights. What's your choice?"

"I don't care anymore. If I live, none of this is worth anything. In the very first place he blackmailed me. I knew better but the money he offered looked good so I didn't care. Then I no longer had a choice, as far as he was concerned. He's threatened to kill me a dozen times if once. What do you want from me?"

"Tabatha?"

"There again, George got greedy. Instead of paying for the drugs he had Tabatha's parents carry across the border, he found out they had jewels from a Jewelry heist so he figured it was fair game to kill Tabatha's dad and let her mother bleed to death. Now he had the drugs, the jewels and a baby. Three for the price of one but he never paid, he just took."

"Where did this happen?"

"Mexican border. They crossed over in a dust storm to meet us on the US side."

The nurse barged in, "Are you people still here? I'm sorry I must ask you to leave."

"What about my plea deal?"

Both Bruce Nichols and Smith left without making any promises. "Steve, you can call in back up to stand watch, then book George. When you are done with that meet us in the coffee shop. We'll still be there."

Stumps phone rang. "Oh, okay. The Turners could meet us at the coffee shop but we will have to play everything by ear. Can't begin to know how everything plays out. Be very cautious, don't know what kind of a reaction Tabatha will have. She's been through a lot."

Chapter Forty-Eight
The Future

Officer Benton turned to Dr. Tim Turner and Anita. "They seem to think we could go to our meeting place. Just be very aware, Tabatha has no idea that you are even looking for her or that you are alive. We couldn't begin to know how she will react."

"I can't expect anything, I guess."

"We'll go in and sit down. You'll be introduced when the undercover cops who have been working on this case decide it is time. It will be better for Tabatha and the both of you."

"I don't get it. How is it that she's involved with the law? What has she done?"

"You will be brought up to date when we get there. Until then, just go with the flow."

Facing the unknown was her overwhelming fear as she waited. Fatigue was beginning to set in. Tim and she had come so far and now her daughter was embroiled with the law. Had she gotten caught up in drugs? Was she unknowingly following into her mother's past? Tim saw the worried countenance and put his arms around her. "We will get through this, Anita. God will be there with us."

Tabatha turned to Marybeth, "I still don't understand why you even came here in the first place. What else do you know that I haven't heard about yet?"

It was so unlike Tabatha to speak up for herself but realizing she had almost been accosted, there had to be a change in her character. "If you really want Bruce, ask him. He's yours, so leave me alone."

"Bruce? You have to be kidding me. He isn't my type."

"Then why are you here?"

"No, Tabatha, I wanted to ask you to come with me, stay with me." Marybeth grabbed Tabatha by the arm again pulling her back to stand out of sight. "I had no idea you were in this kind of trouble. I just came by to say how sorry I was for how I acted. Then I saw the fire and I couldn't let you go in there. If ever you need anything, I know my family would want you to live with us as long as you want. I know you will need a place to live while going to College or at least until you go."

"I'm still in a daze. I'm hoping I can still stay with Ann and maybe help her."

Bruce and Smith drove up to check on how things were progressing and to check on Tabatha. "Ann was taken by the paramedics to the emergency so she could be checked and kept overnight. We'd like you, Tabatha to come with us. If you wish, your friend Marybeth could come with you but that would be up to you. Might be good to have a friend with you."

"Where are we going?" Asked Marybeth.

"Just the coffee shop to settle our nerves. The drinks are on me."

"You don't want to say no to an offer like that. When my boss says something like that, it's almost too good to be true."

"It's not that bad, Bruce."

"Oh yeah?" Steve was a witness to how tight their boss could be. "He might be caring but he's tight. I'm bringing my service dog. He deserves a treat don't you think?"

"That he does, Steve."

"After all that just went down, do you think the coffee shop will still be open?"

"Tabatha, for us they will. It will also help them recover since they have to stay as witnesses to the shooting. Investigators will already be in there to record all of that information." Smith knew how it worked.

"I don't mind if you want to join us, Marybeth. You always know more than I do anyhow."

"I would rather blame other people for telling me stuff I can't keep to myself. Just maybe I've learned. I didn't know the background to anything that I was told. Assumptions always get me into trouble.

Somehow I'd like to grow into a wise person because of all this. Become a counselor. I've certainly learned enough."

"At least you made me aware of information not even Ann wanted me to know. That helped save me in the end."

"Come, let's be on our way." In Officer Benton's patrol car, Tim and Anita drove toward the place when his phone began ringing. "Hello?" He was silent for a few minutes. "That's your suggestion, then? Of course, I can do that, be glad to." He closed his phone. "That was Sergeant Smith. You'll like him when you get to meet him. It might be a bit late by the time you meet Tabatha."

"The time doesn't matter. I just want to finally see my daughter."

"I'm advised to take you to one of our favorite place where officers like to gather to eat, then as soon as they can we'll get another call for us to get this together."

"Officer, if there is anything that Tabatha has gotten herself into, like maybe drugs or whatever. I will gladly pay any fines she might owe."

Anita was insistent, "I just want to meet Tabatha and the lady that took care of her all these years. I need to be released from the sixteen years of not knowing anything about her."

"I can afford to take care of everything." Dr. Tim Turner wanted to step in and make everything right for his wife and her daughter and this woman that took care of Tabatha all these years."

"You won't be meeting Ann at the moment. There has been a house fire so she is now in the hospital."

"House fire? Was Tabatha there?"

"No, she was not, at least when it caught fire. She was there after the fact."

"Will the lady be okay?"

"Yes, she is just merely being checked out at the hospital overnight. I understand she will be okay."

Officer Benton continued, "Just let's have dinner together because I know the delay won't be long. They're wrapping everything up now."

Anita sat looking at Tim. "Are you really sure? Do you still want to do this?"

"I am. I want to walk through this with you. Your testimony inspires me knowing God can perform the impossible. You are an example of someone who already has proved what our Savior can do for us. This last mile will be completed sooner than you think."

"Please enjoy your dinner. The crew is merely sorting everything out so that when you get there, it will be just a little easier."

Anita picked at her food for her stomach was in turmoil.

Officer Benton tried to tone down the nervousness. "We are not but a few blocks from the place we need to be. We're just waiting for everyone to get there. As soon as they do, Sergeant Stumps and Officer Nichols will be calling." Seldom did any police officer involve their clients with details so he kept the conversation light and more about the work the Officers were often involved with. He explained how they worked with Child Protective Services and how they often were able to work out amenable conclusions in most cases.

"Was Tabatha ever one of your cases?"

Before he could answer, his phone rang again. "Hello. Okay, we'll be there." Officer Turner turned to Tim and Anita, "We can be on our way. Let me pay the bill and we will get right over there."

Anita turned to Tim, "I'm scared."

"I'm with you. You will be okay."

The coffee shop was full of uniformed police officers. Officer Benton sat with Tim and Anita at a corner table. Anita looked around, *my daughter, I haven't seen her for sixteen years. Can I recognize her?*

Tabatha asked, "Why so many people? Shouldn't this place be closed for business?"

"They are."

"You mean those people with the officers are undercover?"

"Don't know."

The Barista started serving coffee on the house.

Bruce looked at Smith, "You knew you wouldn't have to pay, right?"

"I didn't, but I'm not surprised."

"Well, Tabatha, thanks for working with us." Stumps shook her hand.

Anita wanted to jump up and run to her, Tim pulled her down. In her mind she knew, *that's my daughter, they called her Tabatha.*

"We wanted to take you out of the situation you were in." Stumps started looking around to see who was present. "Before we disclosed any of the information we are going to go over with you, you need to know that Bruce has been doing *under-cover* work for us for a few years and he was sure he could keep you safe and at the same time catch the two guys that have been doing the drug deals and have killed their opponents over the last couple of decades. They've been eluding us since your birth, Tabatha. We used Bruce because he looked young enough to disguise as a student. If he hadn't done that, we would have taken you out and put you into foster care. That wouldn't have broken the drug ring nor would it stop them from doing the same as always or finding you eventually for their purposes, that being the reason we chose to handle this the way we did."

Anita squeezed Tim's hand. She was aghast. She held her head in her hands.

"We knew if we could keep you safe and still get what we needed, this would be the better way, especially since Bill had already been caught. We also knew he had taken the wrap for the others."

Tabatha and Marybeth sat in disbelief as they listened.

"We had been hot on the trail of these guys and discovered their intent was to trade young girls for money. Tabatha, you were not the first. They were mixed up with peddling drugs and young teenage girls. They always thought you were the prize so they had Ann rear you. The glitch came when they let Bill take the wrap for them. When he was sentenced to jail time they lost the bookkeeper that kept the money laundering on track."

"Now they needed money but with Bill spending his time in jail he couldn't be there to hand over the money he had in his possession for dealing in drugs. George and Sam's pocket book was now running on empty."

Bruce added, "Tabatha, you don't have to worry about them anymore."

"And when they get out where do I hide?"

"We have to push for the death penalty for George. The others were with him because of blackmail but be assured justice will be served. We will see to it."

"Thanks, Sergeant."

Tabatha wasn't done with questions. "How did they get away with keeping me?"

"Ann had been blackmailed as well. They came up with a notarized letter as to the proof of your birth. Then this is the *kicker*. The Notary person, Bill Thomas was a man who'd been blackmailed by George. They had the information correct for obvious reasons. They were there shortly after you'd been born. Sam is in serious condition in the hospital but we were able to talk with him and gave him some options if he gave us information."

"Ann is really not my mother. She just told me that when they took her to the hospital. Then I heard George say my parents died in a shoot-out."

Everyone sat there listening when Bruce motioned for the other couple to join the group.

"Other people have been frantically looking for you as well. We only just got word that someone was looking for you a few weeks ago." Smith turned to Dr. Tim and Anita.

Anita was in tears, as Tim did the talking. After introductions, Tim continued. "We've been frantically looking for you for all of your sixteen years. Every time we would get closer to your whereabouts, the three men picked up and left. It was no secret that he knew the law was closing in on him."

Bruce added, "This time it was a little different, we now think it was George who framed Bill for a killing we think he committed and of course didn't want to pay the penalty. His fall guy was Bill. Unfortunate for him, with Bill locked up, the money ran dry. The firearms and the schedules for drugs were not anymore available to them. Now they became desperate. That was what we needed."

Anita added, "Unfortunately, Tabatha, your father and I wanted the American Dream. I wasn't happy about it but I was young and stupid. I went along with all of it."

"Anita was able to get her American Citizenship so when we had that worked out we started off in earnest to find you."

Tabatha was stunned. "I don't know what to say."

"Tim has a Shelter near the border town where I was taken after I survived the ordeal. God saw fit to save me, not only my life, but my soul as well."

Bruce interjected, "On the lighter side, your daughter has worked very hard and at sixteen years of age, has earned a four-year scholarship to enter the University of her choice."

"Is Sam okay?"

"It appears, Tabatha, he is in critical condition but could pull through. Don't know how that will go just yet."

"George isn't talking, like that will help him but he has been booked and will be charged with abduction, blackmail and first degree murder." Steve had already accomplished the booking.

"Murder?"

"He killed Ann's husband. She didn't know that. He blackmailed her into believing he was her rescuer. She had no way of knowing."

Tabatha said, "She told me someone killed her husband but George showed up and told her not to talk or she might be accused of her husband's murder." Tabatha hesitated, "Can't believe I didn't pick up on that, of course she isn't my mother or she would have told me earlier."

"George did that so he could use her for his alibi should he need one."

"What happens to Sam?"

"He will also be charged because he is an accessory to the crime, Tabatha."

Bruce added, "Before we even knew at this end that your mother had survived the ordeal, with the lab work we did manage to get your DNA. If you remember Tabatha, I bought a coffee cup for you but then I didn't anymore have it the next time we went for coffee? That's the reason we were finally able to find who you are. Then, like out of thin air, who gives us a call but Officer Benton when Dr. Tim and Anita came asking for his help to find her daughter."

"Apparently, some wise border patrol officers had obtained Anita's DNA when she was taken to Dr. Tim's hospital."

Anita added, "We were at your school because I saw in the papers who was in the graduating class and saw your name. When we got there, it was surrounded with cops. They pulled us out and put us in house arrest. Can you believe that?"

"Sorry, I had to do that. We had an anonymous call that something could go down during the ceremonies. When we arrived, George and Sam were there but when they saw all the Patrol cars they took off but only after we put the school on lock-down. We knew then wanted Tabatha."

Sergeant Smith continued, "We also were able to come up with a biographical history for you and pictures from a file we obtained from the town next to the border. They were left there after your birth when your Mother was taken to the hospital. You'll want to share them with your mother, I'm sure. Here, they are yours."

Tabatha trembled as she took the envelope. "This is my mother and father?"

"That's right and apparently the border patrol officer was able to get your mother's ring for you as well. The police report said that your dad died from gunshot wounds but your mother was taken to the hospital expecting that she would die from complications of childbirth. Obviously your mother survived. You were born in the desert not near any hospital. The pictures of you are in the desert in the middle of a severe dust storm."

"You found my ring? I thought George had taken that as well. Tabatha, please keep that, it's yours."

"Oh, please, can I? May I call you Mother?"

"Of course." They clung to one another.

Bruce looked at Tabatha as she tried to comprehend the information she had been given. "Maybe this will put together your past. It appears you have been given a wonderful step Father and your very own Mother. You need to thank Sergeant Smith. He is the only one who delights in going the extra mile for a kid like you."

"If I could have done more, I would have. One more thing you should know. It appears both your parents are from Sweden, is that correct, Anita?"

"You nailed it. That's where I am from. Sometimes I think I still have a little of the accent. You did have a wonderful Father, Anita. We were young, had no family but Anton really wanted that American Dream. He couldn't have it and I struggled to get it. I only hope that I can keep it."

Smith answered confidently, "We have enough on George that we don't need to bring you into the picture, Anita. He's the murderer. Everyone else was blackmailed and framed. There is no evidence of anything else. That's the case as we see it."

"I don't know what to say. Thanks for each of you caring enough to be in my life in a time like this. I am so grateful. You obviously risked your lives for me. I also thank God that he gave me a clear mind and for giving me each of you. Still I think, Bruce, you could have been killed because of me."

Bruce had another dilemma, he knew his heart would ache for her, but how could he let her disappear. After all this, she surely would never want to have anything to do with him. If he could stay friends with her, maybe then sometime in the future, she would see him differently.

He would have to become more than just a police officer. Would she even want that?

"Tabatha, it's the least I could do for you. I would like to stay in touch and at least enjoy a continued friendship."

"Thank you so much for helping me. I could not have gotten through this without your help and trust. I have to thank you, Marybeth, I would be dead now if you hadn't stopped me. You might have seemed to be my worst nightmare but you proved to be my dearest and best friend."

Bruce said, "I'm glad it didn't come to that, that would've been bad. Thanks for saving Tabatha, Marybeth. You are an awesome kid!"

"I don't deserve the thanks, but it was the least I could do."

"The way I see it, Tabatha, you have a few choices. I have a lot of room in my house where you could stay. In fact, you could house sit while I have to be away for a few months. You'd have the house to yourself."

"But Bruce, she could stay with me. We have lots of room for Tabatha and my parents would be delighted for the pleasure of having her."

Tabatha was more interested in Ann. What will happen to Ann now that this is all over? "I have to take care of Ann. I owe it to her. I just don't know how."

"There could even be a solution for that dilemma. She should be released from the hospital probably tomorrow. We have the money we confiscated, and there is quite a bundle. She should still be able to work at the bar at the moment."

"But where would we live? There is no house anymore."

"You'd never want to go back there anyhow. The both of you can stay at my place until you are able to find a house. Like I said before, Tabatha, I have connections. That would be a lady realtor that owes me one."

Sergeant Smith wasn't done. "Here is another proposition for you to consider. While you are in College, and I have no idea what you would want to study but we would be very interested in having you part time on our investigation team. That is if you had any interest in that direction. Maybe you don't but that is a good part time job offer."

Anita and Tim had heard about enough. "We can help in all of these situations. The woman that reared my daughter will be given anything and everything she should need. If she wishes, even the job of her choice. We could do nothing less, right Tim?"

"Absolutely, Tabatha, please let us be your parents? We've had a life time of searching for you, can you be our daughter? We'll help you with your College choice and anything you want is yours."

Tabatha just sat there dumbfounded. "This is a lot for me."

Bruce wasn't done, "Don't forget about me, I want you to be my friend, at least. Then with your parents' permission, how about a date sometime now that we are on neutral ground? Don't want an answer now. Just think about it."

Tabatha looked at Anita and Tim. They gave her a nod of approval. Then looked at him, again, but her gaze didn't vanish. "Please forgive me. You look different now that I know who you are. I'd consider a date, in the future."

"Believe me, Tabatha, when I get back, it's a date then?"

"I'll entertain that thought."

END

AUTHOR BIOGRAPHY

Diana Linn was born to an American Father and a Mother born in Siberia before the Russian Revolution. Her parents met in Winnipeg, Manitoba where Diana and her siblings were born. Diana and her husband are now resident in Tucson, Arizona.

Diana has a passion for writing and has recently written and published *Can Anyone Tell Me*. More recently, *What If ... The Romanov Dynasty*, a historical mystery; as well as *Abducted & Lost*, a murder mystery.

Each one of her novels have a distinct message that can be seen throughout the story allowing the reader to experience the journey of God's leading.

A BETTER WAY

Romans 3:23
"For everyone has sinned; we all fall short of God's glorious standard.'

Romans 6:23
For the wages of sin is death, but the free gift of God is eternal life through Christ Jesus our Lord.

John 1:12
But to all who believed him and accepted him, he gave the right to become children of God.

Romans 10:9-10
"If you confess with your mouth that Jesus is Lord and believe in your heart that God raised him from the dead, you will be saved. 10 For it is by believing in your heart that you are made right with God, and it is by confessing with your mouth that you are saved."

John 3:18
"There is no judgment against anyone who believes in him. But anyone who does not believe in him has already been judged for not believing in God's one and only Son.
(all taken from the New Living Translation of the Bible)

My advice to you: Find a Godly church with a biblical Pastor that can disciple you if you do not attend a church already.

God Bless,

Diana E. Linn
Author